Dedicated to Carl von Ossietzky and P.M.

Design and layout by: datariot, Straßburger Straße 41, 10405 Berlin (Germany)
Cover photography by: pip/photocase.com
Herstellung und Verlag: Books on Demand GmbH, Norderstedt, 2010

Bibliographical index: (1) societal verification (2) Nuclear Weapons Convention (3) security policy (4) citizen reporting (5) whistleblowing
ISBN: 978-3-8370-6582-4

Distributed by the German Section of IALANA, Schützenstraße 6a, 10117 Berlin (Germany)

This publication was generously supported by Berghof Foundation Research Center for Constructive Conflict Management, Altensteinstraße 48a, 14195 Berlin (Germany)

Dieter Deiseroth

Societal Verification
2nd edition

Citizen Reporting and Whistleblowing as integral elements of the
disarmament process and of technological and other verification systems

2010

Contents

Preface

The threat of nuclear weapons will obviously exist as long as nuclear weapons exist.

The establishment of a nuclear weapons free world requires an international treaty as a permanent and binding structure and an effective regime of verification of compliance with the terms of the respective treaty.

Among those citizens and politicians who are convinced that a nuclear weapons free world is desirable, there are many persons who are concerned about the effectiveness of any treaty to eliminate all nuclear weapons and of any regime of verification in protecting against cheating, such as concealment of a clandestine nuclear arsenal or undetected production of weapons after the treaty enters into force. These concerns apply to the whole spectrum of existing verification methods:

— satellite monitoring and aerial reconnaissance
— remote sensing: visible light (spezial cameras), infrared (heatsensing), radar, synthetic aperture radar (SAR)
— seismology (detecting waves travelling through the earth)
— near-site inspection (monitoring of air, water etc near a plant or facility that might be manufacturing or storing or using nuclear weapons)
— inventory control and verification of records (monitoring of the flow of fissionable materials; records of material balances)
— literature searches of scientific papers to discover the early record of incipient new technology that could be applied to wartime use
— budgetary analysis (inferences as to new military spending not accounted for by known weapons production programs might point to secret or illicit productions)

— on-site inspection in various forms
  » only declared facilities to be inspected or anything the inspectors decide
  » periodically (regularly or at irregular intervals) or continuously (at any time)
  » on challenge (when suspected)
  » pre-announced or by surprise
  » bilateral/mutual or by a third neutral party or by an spezial international organization

I agree with Joseph Rotblat who pointed out many times that the effectiveness of these verification techniques is likely to be greatly improved in the future, if more research effort is put into it, particularly if the weapon designers themselves were given the task of seeking such improvements, as part of the process of conversion of military research establishments to peaceful applications.

Nevertheless, because the above mentioned existing verification techniques and methods have inherent loopholes an additional system of verification would be useful: societal verification which should be an integral part of the disarmament process and of different verification systems.

This booklet contains reprints of two papers (written by the author) and of the respective chapters of the Model Nuclear Weapons Convention (drafted by an international team of law experts and presented by Costa Rica and Malaysia to the UN) concerning the important role of societal verification in its two main forms:

(1) citizen reporting, which relies upon members of civil society (journalists, NGOs, think tanks, universities, mass media), and

(2) whistleblowing by insiders (scientists, technicians, employees, others) working in the relevant disciplines, departments or industries who are encouraged and willing to report to the public or to the national or international verification regime regarding violations of the respective treaty of which they have become aware.

Societal verification with its need for effective protection of individual responsibility can build confidence in state adherence to obligations under a Nuclear Weapons Convention and other national and international verification systems.

Dr. Dieter Deiseroth — Düsseldorf/Leipzig, September 2008

Societal verification: wave of the future?

SOCIETAL VERIFICATION has been discussed for decades under different names, like 'citizens' reporting', 'inspection by the people' and 'social monitoring'. Although there is no agreed legal definition, societal verification connotes the involvement of civil society in monitoring national compliance with, and overall implementation of, international treaties or agreements. One important element is citizens' reporting of violations or attempted violations of agreements by their own government or others in their own country. This encompasses the monitoring of implementation of national legislation or regulations designed to facilitate treaty compliance. A more recent development is civil society monitoring of global compliance with international agreements. In contrast to official verification organisations employing professional experts, societal verification may involve the whole of society or groups
within it.

Whistleblowing is a specific type of citizens' reporting. It relies on violations or attempted violations of an international accord being detected directly by employees, such as scientists and technologists, working in relevant industries.[1] Compared with normal citizens, employees are in a special situation because they owe their employer a certain loyalty and, by law, are normally not allowed to disclose internal or confidential information. Whistleblowers, therefore, need protection if they make a disclosure in good faith and on the basis of reliable evidence. Societal verification may be applied to a wide variety of international agreements (and corresponding national regulations), including those pertaining to the environment, human rights, trade, labour, arms control and disarmament. But the requirements for, and problems of, societal verification in these areas are different. As a result, it is hard to develop a general model of societal verification and its implementation. To begin with, there are discrete actors to be monitored, including:

— commercial and non-commercial companies;
— government departments and agencies;
— various parts of the 'military/industrial complex';
— public and private laboratories;
— public and private research and development centres;

---

*   *first published in: Trevor Findlay <Ed.>, Verification Yearbook 2000, London, 2000, p. 265 – 280*

1   *Joseph Rotblat, 'Societal Verification', in Joseph Rotblat, Jack Steinberger and Bhalchandra Udgaonkar (eds.), A Nuclear-Weapon-Free World: Desirable? Feasible?, Westview Press, Boulder, Colorado, 1998, p. 112.*

— police and security forces;
— national governments; and
— international organisations.

There are also diverse aggregations of interest, influence and power to be handled. Consequently, the implementation of societal verification in disparate areas requires different types of coalition-building and separate forms of regulation and organisation. Varying degrees of transparency and assorted types of whistleblower protection are also necessary.

A short history of societal verification

The first concepts of societal verification were products of the Cold War, when scientists advocated arms control, disarmament and transparency as alternatives to the danger of nuclear deterrence. In the late 1950s, Lewis Bohn[2] and Seymour Melman[3] proposed the idea of 'Inspection by the people'. Their belief was that, in addition to monitoring by the official inspectorate of an international disarmament agreement, it would be useful to have an informal network based on public involvement. This could reinforce the work of the inspectorate and help undercut evasion efforts. Since illicit production of banned weapons would require substantial organisations and production systems the chances were that someone would eventually 'blow the whistle'.

Bohn and Melman argued that disarmament agreements should make it an explicit obligation of citizens to report violations to the international inspectorate. Members of the inspectorate would have the chance to participate in the work of universities and similar institutions of the host country. Additionally, special agreements to guarantee the security of those who co-operated with the inspectorate should be reached (such as facilitating political asylum and temporary local security). Lewis Bohn called specifically for a provision in arms control agreements requiring all participating governments to make it a crime to violate provisions of the accord or to keep secret from the international verification agency any information about such a contravention.[4] These provisions should be

---

2   Lewis Bohn, *Memorandum of 12 January 1956 to the RAND Corporation (not published); reproduced in Lewis Bohn, 'Tecniche d'ispezione non materiale', in: Donald G.Brennan (ed.), Controlli degli armamenti, disarmo e sicurezza nazionale, New York/Milan 1961, p. 466.*

3   Seymour Melman, *'General Report', in Seymour Melmon (ed.), Inspection for Disarmament, Columbia University Press, New York, 1958, p. 38.*

4   Lewis Bohn, *'Non-Physical Inspection Techniques', in Donald G. Brennan (ed.), Arms Control, Disarma-*

publicised by each government and failure to support them by such publicity (or in other ways) would be a major
violation of the treaty.

In the early 1960s, Grenville Clark and Louis Sohn mentioned the concept of 'inspection by the people' in their classic book, World Peace Through World Law.[5] They proposed a revision of the UN Charter to establish a UN Inspection Service. An Annex dealing with citizens' reporting would read:[6]

... Any person having any information concerning any violation of this Annex or any law or regulation enacted thereunder shall immediately report all such information to the United Nations Inspection Service. The General Assembly shall enact regulations governing the granting of rewards to persons supplying the Inspection Service with such information, and the provision of asylum to them and their families ... No nation shall penalise directly or indirectly any person or public or private organisation supplying information to the United Nations with respect to any violation of this Annex. ...

Leo Szilard[7] considered the concept of 'inspection by the people' in his quixotic story The Voice of the Dolphins, published in 1961. He incorporated elements of the proposals of Bohn and Melman and suggested an award of one million dollars, tax free, to be paid by the government accused of a violation. This would be returnable if the information later turned out to be incorrect.

These early concepts of 'inspection by the people' had a double function. First, they were clearly aimed at reducing opposition to arms control and general and complete disarmament by showing that it was possible to verify such agreements through non-official means. Second, they tried to show that, from a democratic point of view, security matters were too important to leave to politicians and military commanders and their staffs alone. These concepts were raised in public debate and were, in turn, influenced by it. They also reflected the technological possibilities of the period. Proponents had to de-

---

ment, and National Security, Braziller, New York, 1961.

5   *Greenville Clark and Louis Sohn (eds.), World Peace Through World Law, Harvard University Press, Cambridge Massachusetts, 2nd ed., 1962, p. 264.*

6   *Clark and Sohn, p. 267.*

7   *Leo Szilard, The Voice of Dolphins, Simon and Schuster, New York, 1961. In 1946, Szilard organised a campaign of scientists against a US government plan (May–Johnson Bill) to subject all nuclear research to a special agency.*

fend themselves against the criticism that 'inspection by the people' would increase the danger of espionage and that such ideas were utopian, since the countries on the other side of the 'Iron Curtain' would never comply with them.

In the 1990s, Joseph Rotblat, in particular, took up these old ideas and applied them to the concept of a treaty on the complete elimination of nuclear weapons.[8] He suggested that the duty of the citizen to supply information about any violation should be an integral part of the accord. Disclosing data about sensitive national security matters to an international body in regard to a treaty violation would, therefore, no longer be considered a crime or an act of treason, but be sanctioned by domestic law. Rotblat pointed out that apart from relying on their ad hoc observations, scientists and technologists could establish organisations to act as compliance watchdogs, monitoring the activities of individuals likely to become involved in an illegal project. Such monitoring could be done, without appearing to spy on one's colleagues, by keeping a register of scientists and technologists and noting changes in their place of work or pattern of publications (or their absence). Other signs of attempted clandestine activities would include: the commencement of new projects at academic institutions without proper justification; the recruitment of young scientists and engineers in numbers not warranted by the declared purpose of the project; or the large-scale procurement of certain types of apparatus, materials and equipment.

All establishments dealing with nuclear facilities, such as those processing and storing spent fuel elements from nuclear reactors or enrichment plants, should be subject not only to monitoring by the International Atomic Energy Agency (IAEA), but also by watchdog organisations.[9]

Challenges facing societal verification

There is a widespread view that in non-democratic countries with little respect for individual human liberties and rights, citizens' reporting and whistleblowing are likely to be ineffective. Yet, reporting by civil rights groups and other non-governmental organisations (like Amnesty International, Human Rights Watch and the Bellona Foundation[10])

---

8   *Rotblat, p. 107.*

9   *Rotblat, p. 114.*

10   *For instance, see the case of Alexander Nikitin, former captain of the Soviet navy, who reported on the Russian Northern Fleet and the sources of radioactive contamination in 1995 and 1996. See his study, Sources*

has for many years played an important role in strengthening compliance with international agreements even in non-democratic states, especially in the areas of human rights and the environment. Amnesty International's reports are an important resource for anyone monitoring state behaviour with respect to human rights. Even in a non-democratic system, a government cannot be absolutely sure that persons with knowledge of clandestine activities will not transmit the information to the international community. Examples include the son-in-law of Iraqi President Saddam Hussein, General Hussein Kamal Hassan, who, in 1991, disclosed Iraq's calutron purchases and other clandestine nuclear and biological weapon activities, first to the US, and, later, to the UN Special Commission (UNSCOM).[11] Another case is that of Russian chemist Vil Mirzajanow, who reported on the secret chemical weapon activities of the former Soviet Union.[12]

A treaty for which societal verification could be particularly powerful is the 1972 Biological Weapons Convention (BWC). Although the BWC bans the acquisition and use of biological weapons, it does not prohibit scientists from conducting research on substances that, although useful for peaceful purposes, are also potentially relevant to the development of biological weapons.[13] Indeed, it is difficult to draw an exact line between research and development of biological and toxin weapons and activities with peaceful motives. There is little doubt that a small group of people, even in government, could produce biological weapons without being detected.[14] Citizens' reporting and, especially, whistleblowing could have an important role to play, as demonstrated by Russian defector Kanathan Alibekow (alias Ken Alibek[15]), who, in 1992, revealed the existence of Biopreparat, the network of clandestine Russian biological weapon research centres.[16]

---

of Radioactive Pollution in the Murmansk and Archangelsk Regions, and his special Bellona Report.

11   See Tim Trevan, Saddam's Secrets, Harper Collins, London, 1999.

12   See Vil Mirzayanow, 'It's time to release my mentor', speech to the 'Democracy, Human Rights and Mordechai Vanunu' international conference, Tel Aviv, Israel, 14–15 October 1996 (unpublished). For further information, see 'A poisoned policy', Moscow News Weekly, no. 39/1992, p. 9; Frank von Hippel, 'Russian Whistleblower Faces Jail', Bulletin of the Atomic Scientists, March 1993, p. 7; New Times International, 45/1992, p. 22; Reiner Braun, Angeklagt wegen 'Geheimnisverrats', in Wissenschaft und Frieden, 1/1994, pp. 71–72.

13   See the chapter by Robert J. Mathews in this volume.

14   See Wolfgang Fischer (Research Centre Jülich), 'Learning from Other Regimes: Social Monitoring as a Contribution to Effective Safeguards?', in Proceedings of the Seminar on Modern Verification Regimes: Similarities, Synergies and Challenges, Helsinki, 12–14 May 1998, p. 119.

15   Frankfurter Allgemeine Zeitung, 3 November 1999.

16   Ken Alibek with Stephen Handelman, Biohazard, Random House, New York, 1999; Judith Miller, 'Aid is Diverted to Germ Warfare, Russian Scientists Say', New York Times, 25 January 2000, available at www.nytimes.com.

The same is true for the arms trade and exports of embargoed 'dual use' technology. Illicit transfers of nuclear, chemical and additional materials to Iraq from the UK and other countries between 1980 and 1990, in violation of the UN arms embargo, are illustrative. In one case, an employee of the British company, Matrix Churchill, wrote to the UK Foreign Secretary warning that equipment was being exported illegally to Iraq. Although his letter was ignored by civil servants for a number of years, it was ultimately the fear that he would contact the press that caused the UK Deputy Prime Minister to reveal that the government had been aware of the exports.[17]

Whistleblowers like Alibekow and Mirzajanow are part of a long tradition. One of the most famous examples is that of the German Nobel Peace Prize Laureate, Carl von Ossietzky, a journalist and writer in the 1920s and 1930s. In his periodical *Die Weltbühne*,[18] he disclosed secret military co-operation between the German army and the Soviet authorities, which violated the international agreements concerning disarmament measures in the 1919 Versailles Peace Treaty. He was convicted of treason and espionage and imprisoned.[19]

Some observers assert that societal verification smacks too much of the mythical 'Big Brother' society, wherein citizens watch each other and the state watches citizens. Societal verification, however, aims, by definition and design, for openness and the free flow of ideas. It can substantially extend the information base of official verification efforts and contribute to the protection of democratic rights. One of the most difficult aspects of societal verification and its special form of whistleblowing is that it implies disloyalty, the stigma of spying on one's colleagues. The tension between an organisation's concern to control its own affairs and the public's interest in knowing of developments which violate international agreements is often mirrored in a tension of loyalties among its professional employees. Professionals working in large organisations often make early assessments of the adverse impact of science and technology on society. But such organisations are generally eager to avoid the 'premature' disclosure of concerns that may later be unsubstantiated. Management often sees dissenting employees as challenging the legitimacy of its authority, while whistleblowing is viewed as a challenge to the credibility of the

17   Guy Dehn, 'Project Whistleblowing—The UK experience', working paper, Public Concern at Work, London, 2000, p. 14.

18   Published on 12 March 1931 in the Weltbühne ('Windiges aus der deutschen Luftfahrt').

19   For further information, see Ingo Müller, Der Weltbühnenprozeß von 1931, in: Carl von Ossietzky, 227 Tage im Gefängnis. Luchterhand Literatur Verlag, Darmstadt, 1988, p. 13.

organisation as a whole. Dissent may, therefore, cause confrontation between the individual expert and management. For many employees this is too intimidating a prospect. The stigma of disloyalty would be reduced, however, if these activities were protected and positively sanctioned by international and domestic law.

The suppression of professional dissent can itself have damaging effects on an organisation by straining the loyalty, morale and creativity of employees and the credibility and reputation of the organisation. Dissent is often an early sign of problems that may escalate into serious and expensive crises if not dealt with early and effectively.

First steps towards societal verification

In recent years several encouraging steps have been taken in the direction of societal verification at the international and national levels, but much remains to be done.

Societal verification provisions of the Model Nuclear Weapons Convention In 1997, an international consortium of lawyers, scientists and disarmament specialists—co-ordinated by the US Lawyers' Committee on Nuclear Policy—drafted a Model Nuclear Weapons Convention (Model NWC).[20] At the request of Costa Rica, it was circulated as a UN document. Article VIIB states that 'persons shall report any violation of this Convention to the Verification Agency established by the Convention'. This responsibility takes precedence over any obligation not to disclose information that may exist under national security laws or employment contracts. Data received by the Agency will be held in confidence, except to the extent necessary for investigative purposes, until formal charges are lodged. Article VIIC deals with both intrastate and interstate protection. It proposes the following intra-state provisions:

— 'Any person reporting a suspected violation of this Convention, either by a person or a State, shall be guaranteed full civil and political rights including the right to liberty and security of person';

20　*UN Document A/C.1/52/7, 17 November 1997. For additional information, see Security and Survival: The Case for a Nuclear Weapons Convention, International Association of Lawyers Against Nuclear Arms/ International Network of Engineers and Scientists Against Proliferation/International Physicians for the Prevention of Nuclear War, Cambridge, Massachusetts, 1999. The Model NWC can be downloaded from www. ippnw.org.*

- states parties 'shall take all necessary steps to ensure that no person reporting a suspected violation of this Convention shall have any rights diminished or privileges withdrawn as a result';
- any individual who, in good faith, 'provides the Agency or a National Authority with information regarding a known or suspected violation of this Convention cannot be arrested, prosecuted or tried on account thereof ';
- 'It shall be an unlawful employment practice for an employer to discriminate against any employee or applicant for employment because such person has opposed any practice as a suspected violation of this Convention, reported such violation to the Agency or a National Authority, or testified, assisted, or participated in any manner in an investigation or proceeding under this Convention'; and
- 'Any person against whom a national decision is rendered on account of information furnished by such person to the Agency about a suspected violation of this Convention may appeal such decision to the Agency within . . . months of being notified of such decision. The decision of the Agency in the matter shall be final.'

The interstate section includes a provision that, 'any person reporting a violation of this Convention to the Agency shall be afforded protection by the Agency and by all States Parties, including, in the case of natural persons, the right of asylum in all other States Parties if their safety or security is endangered in the State Party in which they permanently reside'.

Other provisions state that the Executive Council established by the Convention 'may decide to award monetary compensation to persons providing important information to the Agency concerning violations of this Convention'. In addition, 'Any person who voluntarily admits to the Agency having committed a violation of this Convention, prior to the receipt by the Agency of information concerning such violation from another source, may be exempt from punishment. In deciding whether to grant such exemption, the Agency shall consider the gravity of the violation involved as well as whether its consequences have not yet occurred or can be reversed as a result of the admission made'.

Civil society 'second track' monitoring: Landmine Monitor

The 1997 Landmine Convention does not have a standing verification mechanism.[21] In September 1998, however, non-governmental organisations (NGOs) involved in the International Campaign to Ban Landmines (ICBL) set up Landmine Monitor, a civil society-based reporting network for monitoring state compliance.[22] For many years, NGOs and research centres, like the Stockholm International Peace Research Institute (SIPRI), have monitored compliance with international treaties informally and individually. But Landmine Monitor is the first attempt to create a systematic, global non-governmental monitoring network. Although Landmine Monitor has no official status under the treaty, its reports cover every aspect of implementation and compliance by all countries, as well as thematic issues. The first report was presented to the First Meeting of States Parties in Maputo, Mozambique, in May 1999, while the second was presented to the Second Meeting of States Parties in Geneva, Switzerland, in September 2000.[23]

US whistleblower protection

The Federal Whistleblower Protection Act (5 USC sec. 1201), which became effective on 9 July 1989, gives federal employees protection by forbidding government agencies from acting against any employee for declining to engage in illegal activity.[24] The Act also covers activities banned by international (self-executing[25]) treaties to which the US is a party. Under Article VI of the US Constitution, a treaty that has been adopted with the consent of two-thirds of the Senate and does not require legislation to implement its provisions domestically, automatically becomes national law. The Act must be seen in the light of the US Government Employees' Code of Ethics, which states that it is the duty

---

21 *The Treaty does, however, require annual reports by states parties on their compliance and outlines the means by which compliance problems could be resolved; these annual reports are published by the UN Secretariat. Additionally, the Treaty provides for annual meetings of states parties to assess its effectiveness.*

22 *See Trevor Findlay, 'Landmine Monitor: Pioneering 'Track Two' Verification', Trust & Verify, no. 83, November 1998, p. 1.*

23 *The 1999 and 2000 Landmine Monitor reports may be found at www.icbl.org.*

24 *See Tom Devine, The Whistleblower's Survival Guide, Government Accountability Project, Washington, DC, 1997, p. 124. More information on the Government Accountability Project and links to other resources on whistleblowing can be found at www.whistleblower.org.*

25 *A self-executing treaty becomes internal law in the US immediately upon entry into force internationally; non-self-executing treaties require legislation to implement them domestically. For further information, see Thomas Buergenthal and Harold Maier, Public International Law, second edition, West Publishing Company, St. Paul, Minnesotta, 1990, p. 204.*

of any person in government service to: 'Put loyalty to the highest moral principles and to country above loyalty to persons, party or Government department' and 'Uphold the Constitution, laws, and regulations of the United States and of all governments therein and never be a party to their evasion'.

The Whistleblower Protection Act did not always live up to its promise. The principal reason was the lack of sufficient evidence connecting the employee's whistleblowing and reprisals by employers.[26] A 1993 survey found that, by a 60–23 margin, federal employees did not believe their rights would be protected. The rate of retaliation by superiors for whistleblowing was 37 percent; 45 percent reported that acting on their rights landed them in more trouble.[27] Agencies and agency bodies responsible for the Act's implementation were unwilling to enforce it. The Act was amended in 1994, offering significant improvements.[28] Federal employees covered by collective bargaining agreements now receive state-of-theart administrative law protection through arbitration hearings. They can seek immediate relief through legal action to stop temporarily the adverse personnel action and can sue managers who attempt reprisals. Employees can prove the connection between whistleblowing and reprisal simply by demonstrating, for instance, a short time lapse between the whistleblowing and the employee's next performance appraisal. The whistleblower will only have to prove that dissent was a contributing factor in the job action; once this is established, the burden of proof shifts to the agency to prove by 'clear and convincing evidence' that it would have taken the same action anyway on independent grounds. In addition, the amendments require the Merit Systems Protection Board to refer managers for disciplinary investigations whenever there is a finding that reprisal was a contributing factor in action taken against personnel.

In contrast to the US federal public sector, there is no comprehensive law that prohibits employers in the private sector from retaliating against whistleblowers. But some states have adopted common law remedies under the 'public policy exception to the termination at will doctrine'. Today, 42 states and the District of Columbia offer protection to employees who suffer discrimination for blowing the whistle on an issue of importance to the public, such as health or safety. But there are no general or specific provisions that

---

26 *See General Accounting Office, 'Determining Whether Reprisal Occurred Remains Difficult', GGD-93-3, 27 October 1992, Washington, DC, cited in Gerald Caiden and Judith Truelson, 'An Update on Strengthening the Protection of Whistleblowers', Australian Journal of Public Administration, vol. 53, 1994, p. 575.*
27 *See Devine, p. 128; Caiden and Truelson, p. 579.*
28 *See Devine, p. 129; Dieter Deiseroth, Berufsethische Verantwortung in der Forschung. Möglichkeiten und Grenzen des Rechts, LIT-Verlag, Münster, 1997, pp. 233 ff.*

protect whistleblowers who make disclosures concerning breaches of an international treaty.

Russia: a right of disclosure?

In recent years there have been many prosecutions of Russian whistleblowers accused of divulging state secrets or even treason or espionage by handing over real or potential state secrets to the public and/or foreign organisations. Examples include the cases of Alexandr Nikitin[29] and Grigorij Pescov.[30]

The Russian Federal Law on State Secrets (no. 5485-1), adopted on 21 July 1993, provides in Article 5 a 'List of information considered as state secrets'. This list was significantly expanded by an amendment adopted on 9 October 1997. It mainly includes military-related information, such as the contents of strategic or operational plans, plans for the Russian armed forces and details of the production of nuclear and other special armaments. Nevertheless, Article 7, which was not significantly changed on 9 October 1997, expressly determines a category of information that cannot be kept secret: 'information on extraordinary events and catastrophes that threaten the safety and health of the population, and the consequences of such events'. The same applies to 'information on the ecological situation'. It is still not clear if, and how, the Russian authorities, especially the criminal and administrative courts, will handle these provisions, which contain elements necessary for the protection of whistleblowers. It will be of great interest to observe further developments in this area in Russia.

The UK Public Interest Disclosure Act

The UK Public Interest Disclosure Act, which came into force on 2 July 1999, protects employees from dismissal and victimisation if they make a 'qualifying disclosure'.[31] The

---

29 *Alexandr Nikitin (St. Petersburg), a former Soviet navy captain, has been prosecuted for high treason and divulging state secrets. He contributed to various studies and publications on potential risks of radioactive pollution in the Murmansk and Archangelsk regions. For further information, see Dieter Deiseroth and Dietmar Göttling (eds.), Der Fall Nikitin/The Nikitin Case, G.Emde-Verlag, Pittenhart, 2000.*

30 *Grigory Pasko, a Russian naval officer and military journalist ('Bojewaja Wachta'), sent controversial reports to Japanese television and newspapers, accusing the Russian navy of spilling nuclear waste into the Sea of Japan. He was arrested in 1997 on his return from Japan and charged with selling state secrets abroad. See Die Zeit, no. 8, 1999, p. 33.*

31 *For further information, see Public Concern at Work (ed.), Current Law Statutes. Public Interest Disclosure Act 1998. Annotations by Guy Dehn, Legal Information Resources, Sweet & Maxwell, London, 1999.*

legislation applies to people at work raising genuine concerns about crime, illegality, miscarriage of justice, danger to health and safety or the environment and the covering up of any of these matters. It applies whether or not the information is confidential and extends to malpractice occurring outside the UK (§43B section 2).

A whistleblower who feels victimised can bring a claim before an employment tribunal for compensation; additionally, if the employee is sacked, he or she may apply for an interim order to keep their job. 'Gagging' clauses in employment contracts and severance agreements are void insofar as they conflict with the Act. The Act makes provision for the following five types of disclosure:

— internal disclosures—made in good faith, to a manager or the employer, if the whistleblower has reasonable suspicion that malpractice has occurred, is occurring or is likely to occur;
— disclosures in government-appointed bodies—if employees report their concerns in good faith directly to the sponsoring department, rather than to their employer;
— regulatory disclosures—made in good faith to regulatory bodies specified under the Act, such as the Health and Safety Executive, Inland Revenue, Customs and Excise, and the Financial Services Authority, if the whistleblower reasonably believes that the information and any allegation in it are substantially true;
— wider disclosures—for instance to the police, the media, Members of Parliament, pressure groups, and non-prescribed regulators. These disclosures are protected, if, in addition to the tests for regulatory disclosures, they are reasonable in the circumstances. But they are not protected if made for personal gain. Furthermore, one of the following tests must be met: the whistleblower reasonably believed that they would be victimised if they raised the matter internally or with a prescribed regulator; they reasonably believed that a cover-up was likely and there was no prescribed regulator; or they had already raised the matter internally or with a prescribed regulator;
— disclosures in exceptionally serious matters—a disclosure will be protected if the concern is exceptionally serious, if it meets the test for regulatory disclosures, and if it is not made for personal gain. The disclosure must also be reasonable, having particular regard for the identity of the person it was made to.

Employees who, for instance, warn a Member of Parliament or the media that munitions are likely to be exported in violation of an arms embargo or an international agreement incorporated into the law of the land, would be able to seek the Act's protection under its 'wider disclosure' or 'disclosure of an exceptionally serious nature' provisions. Only in those cases where a whistleblower was or would have been guilty of breaching the Official Secrets Act or of another secrecy offence by making an external disclosure would the Public Interest Disclosure Act's protection not apply. Overall, though, by setting out a relatively clear framework for raising genuine concerns about crime and illegality and by guaranteeing legal protection to employees who raise such issues, the Act could be an important step in creating a culture favourable to societal verification in the UK.

France: civil society involvement in implementation of Landmine Convention

In France, one example of officially sanctioned citizens' reporting is NGO involvement in the process of implementing the Landmine Convention. The French Act concerning the Abolition of Anti-Personnel Landmines establishes in Article 9 a National Committee to participate in monitoring implementation of the country's obligations under the treaty.[32] Membership of the Committee, besides representatives of the French government and Parliament, will include NGO representatives. Article 10 of the Act states that the National Committee will provide for effective implementation of the Convention and the international activities of the French Republic concerning de-mining and help for victims of anti-personnel landmines. The French government is obliged to report annually to Parliament on the implementation of the Act. While these provisions provide for only limited participation by representatives of civil society in a public body involved in a verification process, the French initiative can be seen as a significant precedent in making societal verification more acceptable and likely.

Future possibilities

To make social verification more likely, the following steps would be helpful:

— the legal right of all citizens and citizen groups to engage in societal verification needs to be guaranteed by each international agreement and by the legal system of each state party;
— explicit legal protection against discrimination and criminal prosecution should be established for all (natural and legal) persons reporting violations or attempted violations of an international agreement;

---

32 'Tendant à l'élimination des mines antipersonnel', *Journal Officiel de la République Francaise*, 9 July 1998, p. 10456.

— the right to raise funds for citizens' verification purposes, within and outside the country, must be guaranteed so that citizen groups obtain financial resources for their work; and
— regulations concerning freedom of information and openness in science should be promulgated.

Freedom of information means that records in the possession of public agencies and departments of the executive branch are accessible to citizens. Those seeking information should no longer be required to prove that they are entitled to obtain the data and have a special need for it. Instead, the 'need to know' standard must be replaced by a 'right to know' doctrine. The government or head of the relevant public agency must be required to justify the legally protected need for secrecy (for instance, properly classified documents, internal personal rules and practices, confidential business data, internal government communications, personal privacy and law enforcement). But it should be established, by law, that international and domestic legislation must not protect illegal 'state secrets'. Information on violations of international or domestic law by state officials cannot be kept confidential.

Whistleblowing

Since any serious attempt to violate an international treaty or corresponding national legislation would require the involvement of technologists, scientists and other employees, societal verification is nearly impossible without special protection for those who 'blow the whistle'. Possible initiatives to achieve this include:

— legal protection against discrimination and criminal prosecution for whistleblowers should be established by international treaties and domestic law. Due process protection for dissenting employees should be established by state legislation. It should include the right of all professionals and employees to inform, in good faith, appropriate bodies, or, if necessary, the public, of plans, projects and measures in their workplace or outside their workplace which violate national or international law or principles of professional ethics, and to refuse to work on such projects;
— exemption from punishment in case of self-disclosure (revelation of one's own involvement in forbidden activities) should be guaranteed; and
— international and domestic law should guarantee that a whistleblower can rely on legal protection in foreign countries in case of discrimination or criminalisation by their own state (that is, the right to asylum).

To encourage citizens to 'blow the whistle' as an important element of societal verification, it would also be necessary to establish loyalty to a much larger group than one's own organisation and nation. Universal loyalty to humankind must be developed and strengthened, an important task for the education system and mass media. The responsibility of scientists, technologists and other employees could be developed through training to identify activities that may be prohibited or ethically questionable. Scientists in universities and academies could develop special programmes and curricula for teaching and learning, such as: awareness of ethical problems in research and development; ethically responsible behaviour as a professional and employee; and management of ethical conflicts. It could become an obligatory part of student examinations to scrutinise the possible ethical consequences of scientific and technological proposals, inventions and developments.

Organisations and enterprises could develop due process procedures for dealing with dissent and dissenters in a fair and responsive manner. Initiatives could include: devising a Code of Ethics and Professional Conduct which guarantees that nobody is discriminated against or sanctioned if they make a protected disclosure to a specified internal or external person or body; appointing an ombudsman within the organisation (concerned with ethical behaviour); and establishing a hotline for complaints (anonymous or otherwise).

Additionally, organisations of scientists, technologists and other employees could support and encourage potential and actual whistleblowers, and monitor the activities of individuals and groups likely to become involved in projects contravening international accords, domestic law or standards of professional ethics. They could:

— develop a Model Code of Ethics and Professional Conduct for their membership;
— publicise appropriate whistleblower cases and ethical conflicts;
— publish details of the cases and names of employers who have discriminated against responsible professionals or other ethical employees;
— offer professional advice in actual conflicts;
— organise acts of solidarity with whistleblowers;
— establish ethical support funds;
— award whistleblowers; and
— lobby for better legal protection of whistleblowers.

As to the international arena, an amendment to the UN Charter, as proposed by Clark and Sohn, would only be feasible in exceptional historical circumstances, which have not yet arrived. The idea of including protective clauses for citizens' reporting and whistleblowing in international treaties should prove easier, although it will still be difficult for citizens' groups and other NGOs to achieve.

The technological revolution, meanwhile, especially in the field of communication systems, like the Internet, will facilitate societal verification. But the Internet and other technologies will not remove the need for legislative protection. Employees and other citizens who whistleblow in good faith must still be protected against all forms of pressure, discrimination and retaliation in their workplace and personal and professional environment, and against criminal prosecution by their authorities.

It will likely take many years to establish effective measures of societal verification in international agreements, because there seems to be little enthusiasm among political decision-makers to develop such tools. Nevertheless, the need for societal verification will increase nationally and internationally. Growing national and international networks of public interest groups,[33] lawyers, legislators, journalists and former whistleblowers are available to assist employees in disclosing irregularities. The movement is also achieving success in its drive to force accountability on governments and industries, since they are coming to see whistleblowers as useful bell-wethers of emerging problems. In many countries, whistleblower protection, conforming largely to the UK and US models, will probably continue to be enacted within the next few years. Because of the significant contributions that citizens' reporting and whistleblowing can make, such developments should be encouraged.

---

33 One example is the International Network of Whistleblower Protection Organizations. For further information, see www.whistleblower.org.

Whistleblowing in der Sicherheitspolitik

Anfang März 2003, wenige Tage vor Beginn des US-Krieges gegen den Irak, wurde bekannt, dass US-amerikanische Regierungsstellen unter Bruch völkerrechtlicher Abkommen[1] die Telefone mehrerer UN-Delegationen in New York abgehört und auch deren sonstigen Datenverkehr überwacht hatten.[2] Zweck dieser illegalen Lauschangriffe war es, wie aus einem internen Memorandum des US-Geheimdienstes NSA vom 31. Januar 2003 hervorgeht,[3] Informationen über das künftige Verhalten dieser Staaten im UN-Sicherheitsrat zu gewinnen, um darauf effektiver Einfluss nehmen zu können. Vor allem ging es um die Abstimmung über den von der US-Regierung eingebrachten Resolutionsentwurf zur Billigung eines Krieges gegen den Irak – damals schwankten die im UN-Sicherheitsrat vertretenen Staaten Angola, Kamerun, Chile, Bulgarien, Guinea und Pakistan („Middle Six") noch, ob sie zustimmen oder einen eigenen Vermittlungsvorschlag einbringen sollten.

Die Enthüllungen in der Presse über diese Lauschangriffe in Wohnungen und Büros stützten sich ganz wesentlich auf Informationen von Katharine Gun, Übersetzerin beim britischen Geheimdienst im Government Communications Headquarters (GCHQ) in Cheltenham bei London. Sie lösten weltweit heftige Proteste aus[4] und trugen maßgeblich zur Isolierung der Kriegsbefürworter und zum Scheitern des US-Resolutionsentwurfs im UN-Sicherheitsrat bei. Katharine Gun hatte bei ihrer dienstlichen Tätigkeit Zugang zu dem NSA-Memorandum vom 31. Januar 2003 erhalten, in dem die NSA unter anderem die britische Regierung um Hilfe beim Ausspionieren von UN-Delegationen bat.[5] Als

---

*   *first published in: Blätter für deutsche und internationale Politik, Volume 4/2004, p. 479 – 490*

1   *Das internationale „Wiener Übereinkommen über diplomatische Beziehungen" legt unmissverständlich in seinem Art. 27 für das Verhältnis von diplomatischen Vertretungen zum jeweiligen Gastland fest: „The receiving state shall permit and protect free communication on the part of the mission for all official purposes [...] The official correspondence of the mission shall be inviolable".*

2   *Später kam heraus, dass offenbar auch UN-Generalsekretär Kofi Annan sowie der Leiter der UN-Waffeninspektion im Irak, Hans Blix, ebenso wie sein Vorgänger Robert Butler und die damalige UN-Menschenrechtsbeauftragte Mary Robinson abgehört wurden, vgl. „Süddeutsche Zeitung" (SZ), 1.3.2004, S. 7.*

3   *In dem NSA-Memo („Top Secret") vom 31.1.2003 hieß es dazu: „The Agency is mounting a surge particularly directed at the UN Security Council (UNSC) members (minus US and GBR of course) for insights as to how to membership is reacting to the on-going debate RE: Iraq, [...] the whole gamut of information that could give U.S. policy makers an edge in obtaining results favorable to U.S. goals or to head off surprises"; www. observer.co.uk/iraq/story/0,12239,905954,00.html.*

4   *Vgl. „The Observer", 9.3.2003.*

5   *Das Memo wurde offenbar im Rahmen des von der NSA und ihren Partnergeheimdiensten im Vereinigten Königreich sowie in Australien, Kanada und Neuseeland betriebenen internationalen Abhörnetzwerks „Eche-*

Frau Gun diese Rechtsbrüche nach reiflicher Überlegung publik gemacht und sich anschließend auch gegenüber ihren Vorgesetzten zu ihrem Verhalten bekannt hatte, wurde sie fristlos entlassen und inhaftiert.[6] Ihr drohten mehrere Jahre Freiheitsstrafe wegen Verstoßes gegen den „Official Secrets Act". Dennoch wurde schließlich die Anklage gegen sie Ende Februar 2004 fallen gelassen, nicht zuletzt auf Druck der britischen Öffentlichkeit. Die Regierung Blair fürchtete nach der „Kelly-Affäre" neues Unheil und bestand nicht auf weiterer Strafverfolgung.

David Kelly hatte in den Jahren 2002/2003 – obgleich lange Zeit durchaus Befürworter eines Militärschlages gegen den Irak – mit seinen Insider-Informationen gegenüber dem britischen Sender BBC und der allgemeinen Öffentlichkeit dazu beigetragen, Unwahrheiten in den Verlautbarungen der britischen Regierung zur Rechtfertigung des Irakkrieges aufzudecken.[7] Kelly bezahlte dies letztlich mit seinem Leben, die genauen Hintergründe seines Todes liegen selbst nach Vorliegen des Untersuchungsberichts des von der Blair-Regierung eingesetzten Lordrichters Hutton nach wie vor im Dunkeln und sind Gegenstand weiterer Debatten.[8]

Auch Joe Wilson, der frühere US-Botschafter in Gabun, ging an die Öffentlichkeit, als die Regierung Bush vor dem Irakkrieg wiederholt behauptete, der Irak habe im afrikanischen Niger Uran zu kaufen versucht. Wilson enthüllte aufgrund eigener Recherchen in einem Artikel, dass es diesen angeblichen Irak-Niger-Uranhandel nie gab und dass dies die britische und die US-Regierung auch wussten. Die US-Regierung reagierte auf Wilsons Vorgehen äußert aufgebracht, sah aber kaum Möglichkeiten, gegen ihn persönlich vorzugehen, zumal das US-Recht Bürgern unter bestimmten Voraussetzungen einen gewissen Schutz gegen Repressalien bietet, wenn sie auf Missstände in der Verwaltung aufmerksam machen.[9]

Öffentlich bekannt wurde auch der Fall des australischen Geheimdienstoffiziers Andrew

---

lon" versandt, vgl. „The Observer", 9.3.2002.

6   Vgl. Nick Cohen, Whistling in the wind, „The Observer", 27.7.2003, http://observer.guardian.co.uk/comment/story/0,6903,1006640,00.html.

7   Ebd.

8   Vgl. Heinrich Senfft, Schwierigkeiten bei der Wahrheitsfindung, in: „Blätter", 12/2003, S. 1485 ff; ders., Lord Huttons Waschsalon, in: „Blätter" 3/2004, S. 279 ff.

9   Stattdessen machten Regierungsstellen den Namen von Wilsons Frau publik, die bis dahin als verdeckte CIA-Agentin tätig war und durch die Enthüllung ihrer Identität in eine für sie lebensbedrohliche Situation geriet.

Wilkie. Wilkie enthüllte, dass sich die australische Regierung zur Rechtfertigung ihrer aktiven Teilnahme am Irakkrieg auf gefälschte Geheimdienstbeweise stützte. Gegen ihn entfesselten australische Regierungsstellen daraufhin eine heftige Attacke in den Medien, in denen er unter Verweis auf eheliche Probleme als „durchgedreht" und „geistesgestört" hingestellt wurde.[10]

Diese Whistleblower-Fälle[11] haben den amerikanischen Publizisten Daniel Ellsberg, dem im November 2003 in Berlin der „Whistleblower-Preis" für sein Lebenswerk verliehen wurde,[12] animiert, immer wieder Insider aufzufordern, die „Pentagon Papers des Irakkrieges" publik zu machen.[13] Er knüpfte damit an seine eigenen Erfahrungen an, die bereits mehr als dreißig Jahre zurücklagen, in ihrer dramatischen Dimension und ihrer historischen Bedeutung jedoch von großem aktuellem Interesse sind.

Die Auseinandersetzungen um die „Pentagon Papers"

Im August 1964 war Daniel Ellsberg von Staatssekretär McNaughton, den der damalige Verteidigungsminister Robert McNamara mit der Koordination der US-Strategie in Vietnam beauftragt hatte, ins Pentagon geholt worden. An diesem Arbeitsplatz bekam Ellsberg Zugang zu streng geheimen Daten und Akten („beyond top secret"). 1965 ging Ellsberg im Team des Generalmajors Landsdale, Sonderberater des US-Botschafters in Saigon, nach Südvietnam, wo er bis zum Sommer 1967 alle Provinzen des Landes zu besuchen und in engem Kontakt mit der kämpfenden Truppe über die Ergebnisse

---

10   Vgl. John Goetz, Frank Konopatzki und Monika Wagener, Helden und Schurken – Wer büßt für die Irak-Abhöraffäre, Sendemanuskript des WDR-Magazins „Monitor" vom 4.3.2004, S. 4.

11   Ins Deutsche lässt sich der Begriff des Whistleblowings (wörtlich: „Pfeife blasen") am ehesten mit „Alarm schlagen" übersetzen. Whistleblower sind also „ethische Dissidenten", das heißt Personen mit Zivilcourage, die ungeachtet ihnen möglicherweise drohender nachteiliger Konsequenzen aus gemeinnützigen Motiven die „Alarmglocke" läuten, um auf bedenkliche Ereignisse oder Vorgänge in ihrem Arbeits- oder Wirkungsbereich hinzuweisen und auf Abhilfe zu drängen. Näheres zum Begriff bei Dieter Deiseroth, Zivilcourage am Arbeitsplatz – Whistleblowing, in: „Blätter", 2/2000, S.188-198.

12   Dieser Preis wurde von der VDW, der IALANA und INESPE gestiftet; see Dieter Deiseroth/Annegret Falter (Ed.), Whistleblower-Preis 2003 - Daniel Ellsberg, Berlin, 2004 (ISBN 3-8305-0973-1); Deiseroth/Falter (Ed.), Whistleblower in Gentechnik und Rüstungsforschung - Preisverleihung 2005 an Theodore A. Postol und Arpad Pusztai, Berlin, 2006 (ISBN 978-3-8305-1262-2); Deiseroth/Falter (Ed.), Whistleblower in Altenpflege und Infektionsforschung - Preisverleihung 2007 an Brigitte Heinisch und Liv Bode, Berlin, 2007 (ISBN 978-3-8305-1455-8).

13   Vgl. Daniel Ellsberg, It's time to take risks, in: „The Observer", 10.12.2002; ders., Interview mit E&P Herausgeber Greg Mitchell vom 28.1.2003; ders., Leak against this war, in: „The Guardian", 27.1. 2004; ders., Where are Iraq's Pentagon papers?, in: „Boston Globe", 22.2.2004.

der US-„Pazifizierungsbemühungen" zu berichten hatte. Hierbei wurde ihm klar, wie er später in seinen Memoiren schrieb: „We were not fighting on the wrong site, we were the wrong site."[14] Er verließ Vietnam und kehrte zurück zur RAND-Corporation. Dann kam der Schock der sogenannten Tet-Offensive des Vietcongs am 29. Januar 1968: In nahezu allen Provinzen Südvietnams und in Saigon selbst begannen die Einheiten des Vietcongs zeitgleich militärische Angriffe, so dass die US-Streitkräfte und ihre südvietnamesischen Verbündeten in die Defensive gerieten. Kurz darauf veröffentlichte die „New York Times" eine ihr aus dem Pentagon zugespielte Information, derzufolge der US-Oberbefehlshaber in Vietnam von der US-Regierung eine Aufstockung der US-Truppen in Vietnam um weitere 206 000 Soldaten forderte. Dies löste im Senat und in der amerikanischen Öffentlichkeit empörte Reaktionen aus und beschädigte die Glaubwürdigkeit der Regierung, die zuvor ständig ihre Erfolge in diesem militärischen Konflikt herausgestellt hatte.

Bereits im Juni 1967 hatte US-Verteidigungsminister McNamara, der im Herbst als Präsident zur Weltbank wechselte, im Pentagon eine hochrangige Sonderkommission mit dem Auftrag eingesetzt, für seinen Amtsnachfolger Clark Clifford ein Gesamtspektrum von Optionen für die künftige Vietnampolitik zu erarbeiten. Diese Expertise sollte – gestützt auf interne, zum Teil streng geheime Quellen und Unterlagen – „enzyklopädisch und objektiv" die Entwicklung des amerikanischen Engagements in Vietnam seit 1945 und die Ursachen der sich ausweitenden Verstrickung untersuchen. Dafür stellte das

Pentagon 36 Offiziere, Beamte und Wissenschaftler zur Verfügung, darunter Daniel Ellsberg. Ellsberg befasste sich speziell mit der Vietnampolitik des Präsidenten John F. Kennedy. Bei seiner Arbeit stieß er sehr bald auf die für ihn zentrale Frage: Warum täuschten alle US-Präsidenten seit Harry Truman fortlaufend die Öffentlichkeit und den US-Kongress darüber, was sie jeweils in Indochina taten? Er fand heraus, das dies jedenfalls nicht deswegen geschah, weil Untergebene den Präsidenten täuschten. Mit anderen Worten: Die Präsidenten wussten, was sie taten.

Die Arbeiten an der Pentagon-Studie wurden im Januar 1969 abgeschlossen. Das nur in zwölf Exemplaren existierende Werk umfasste in seinem darstellenden und analytischen Teil etwa 3000 Seiten sowie weitere 4000 Seiten Dokumente, insgesamt 47 Bände. Es

---

14 *Daniel Ellsberg, Secrets. A Memoir Of Vietnam And The Pentagon Papers, Viking Press, 2002; vgl. Daniel Ellsberg, Papers On The War, Simon and Schuster, New York, 1972*

wurde vom Pentagon zur „streng geheimen Dienstsache" erklärt.[15]

Ellsberg ging nach dem Ende seiner Tätigkeit im Pentagon wieder zurück zur RAND-Corporation, blieb jedoch fasziniert von allen Fragen, die mit der Vietnam-Studie verbunden waren, und wollte an diesen weiter arbeiten. Es gelang ihm, einen kompletten Satz der gesamten 47-bändigen Pentagon-Studie zu RAND nach Santa Monica transferieren zu lassen. Nachdem er 1970 in die politische Forschungsabteilung des Massachusetts Institute of Technology (MIT) in Boston gewechselt war, geriet er zunehmend in Kontakt mit Kriegsgegnern und der Bürgerrechtsbewegung. Er beteiligte sich nun auch mehrfach an Studentendemonstrationen gegen den Vietnamkrieg. In einem Leserbrief an die „New York Times" forderte er den Abzug der US-Truppen. Immer stärker reifte in ihm – von seiner Ehefrau Patricia Marx gefördert – die Überzeugung, dass er etwas tun müsse, um den Krieg zu beenden. Im September 1969 erschien in der „Los Angeles Times" ein Artikel, in dem über US-Kriegsverbrechen in Vietnam sowie über die Versuche der Armeeführung berichtet wurde, sie zu vertuschen. Die Lektüre löste schließlich seinen Entschluss aus, die Pentagon-Studie zu veröffentlichen.[16]

Zusammen mit seinem Freund Anthony Russo machte sich Daniel Ellsberg ab dem 1. Oktober 1969 daran, auf einem einfachen Kopiergerät in den Büroräumen einer kleinen Anzeigenagentur Kopien aller 47 Bände der Pentagon-Studie anzufertigen. Jeden Abend trug Ellsberg, der als früherer Mitarbeiter weiterhin Zugang zum Archiv von RAND hatte, die Papiere in seiner Aktentasche aus dem Archiv heraus, fotokopierte sie und brachte sie wieder zurück. Dabei achtete er peinlich genau darauf, jeweils die Kopf- und Fußzeilen der Dokumente abzutrennen, auf denen sich die Top-Secret-Stempel des Pentagons befanden. Anderenfalls wäre eine spätere weitere Vervielfältigung in kommerziellen Copyshops unnötig erschwert worden.

Alle Versuche Ellsbergs, Mitglieder des US-Kongresses in der Folgezeit für die brisante Kopie zu interessieren, blieben erfolglos. Selbst die Senatoren William Fulbright, Gaylord Nelson und George McGovern, der demokratische Präsidentschaftskandidat von 1972, waren nicht bereit, die mit einer Veröffentlichung in den Medien oder in den Kongress-Drucksachen verbundenen politischen und strafrechtlichen Risiken einzugehen. Schließlich wandte sich Daniel Ellsberg – entsprechend einer Empfehlung von Senator

---

15   „History of U.S. Decision-Making Process on Viet Nam Policy"
16   Vgl. Ellsberg, Secrets, a.a.O., S. 300 ff.

McGovern[17] – Anfang März 1971 an Neil Sheehan, einen Journalisten der „New York Times“, der großes Interesse an der Studie zeigte. Der Entscheidungsprozess in den Leitungsgremien der „New York Times“ zog sich über Wochen hin. Als Daniel Ellsberg am 12. Juni 1971 von einem bei der „New York Times“ beschäftigten Freund erfuhr, dass die Zeitung am nächsten Tage mit dem Abdruck einer Serie zur Pentagon-Studie beginnen wollte, geriet er in Panik, weil er deren Beschlagnahme befürchtete. Hastig brachte er ein in seiner Wohnung gelagertes Exemplar der Studie zu einem Bekannten. Zusammen mit seiner Frau tauchte er für die nächsten Tage unter, um dem befürchteten Zugriff des FBI zu entgehen. Am folgenden Tag, dem 13. Juni 1971, erschien tatsächlich in der „New York Times“ – zur großen Überraschung der US-Regierung – der erste Artikel einer Serie, in der große Teile der sogenannten „Pentagon Papers“ publiziert werden sollten. Nachdem die ersten drei Artikel erschienen waren, gelang es der Nixon-Regierung, beim Bundesgericht in New York eine einstweilige Verfügung zu erwirken, mit der der Zeitung unter Strafandrohung jeder weitere Abdruck der „Pentagon Papers“ untersagt wurde – ein Vorgang ohne Beispiel in der US-Geschichte. Die Zeitung stoppte daraufhin sofort die weitere Veröffentlichung, legte aber Rechtsmittel ein.

Anschließend begannen insgesamt 18 weitere Zeitungen mit dem Abdruck von Auszügen aus den „Pentagon Papers“. Ihnen waren diese zwischenzeitlich in Kopie ebenfalls zugespielt worden – von Daniel Ellsberg. Die Nixon-Regierung versuchte daraufhin, auch gegen diese Zeitungen einstweilige Verfügungen zu erwirken. Teilweise hatte sie mit ihrem Begehren Erfolg, meist kam sie jedoch mit ihren Anträgen zu spät, um ein Erscheinen noch zu unterbinden. Immer neue Zeitungsveröffentlichungen der „Pentagon Papers“ erschienen. Dieses „Hase-und-Igel-Spiel“ zwischen den Printmedien und der Regierung geriet so zu einem nationalen und internationalen Medienereignis erster Klasse.

Am 28. Juni 1971, drei Tage vor der Entscheidung des Obersten Bundesgerichts („Supreme Court“), stellte sich Daniel Ellsberg den Bundesbehörden in Boston. Er wurde wegen des Verdachts des Diebstahls und der Spionage in der strafverschärfenden Form der Verschwörung („conspiracy“) in Haft genommen. Als Gesamt-Höchststrafe drohten ihm 115 Jahre Gefängnis. Die festgesetzte Kaution von 50 000 Dollar konnten Ellsberg und seine Frau nicht aufbringen. Ellsbergs Schwiegervater, ein wohlhabender Spielzeugfabrikant, lehnte es ab, mit seinen Mitteln dem Schwiegersohn, der nach seiner Meinung „das Vaterland verraten“ und der „US-Armee in den Rücken gefallen war“, zu helfen.

---

17 Vgl. David Rudenstine, *The Day the Presses Stopped*, University of California Press, 1996, S. 41.

Schließlich sprangen Freunde ein, so dass Ellsberg nicht im Gefängnis auf seinen Prozess warten musste, der erst ein Jahr später vor einem Geschworenengericht in Los Angeles stattfinden sollte. Am 30. Juni 1971 – also nur knapp drei Wochen nach dem Erscheinen des ersten Artikels in der „New York Times" – erging dann die Entscheidung des Supreme Courts: Mit einer 6:3-Mehrheit seiner Richter erklärten sie die von den Gerichten auf Antrag der Regierung ausgesprochenen Publikationsverbote für die „„New York Times" und die „Washington Post" für verfassungswidrig.[18] Die Nixon-Administration hatte damit eine große Niederlage erlitten. Alle dazu bereiten Medien konnten nun den Abdruck ihrer Serien ungehindert fortsetzen. Weltweit wurde dies als großer Sieg für die Pressefreiheit gefeiert. Wesentliche Teile der rund 7 000-seitigen Studie wurden in der Folgezeit in unterschiedlichen Buchfassungen veröffentlicht.[19]

Die historischen Folgen der „Pentagon Papers"

Präsident Nixon und sein Außenminister Henry Kissinger fürchteten, dass Daniel Ellsberg aufgrund seiner langjährigen Tätigkeit im Pentagon und bei RAND neben den publizierten „Pentagon Papers" noch weitere Dokumente besitzen und veröffentlichen könnte, die nicht nur die Vorgänger-Präsidentschaften, sondern auch unmittelbar die Nixon-Administration betrafen. Deshalb sollte Daniel Ellsberg – in der aus den illegalen Abhörbändern des Weißen Hauses bekannten Diktion Kissingers „der gefährlichste Mann in Amerika" – kaltgestellt werden. Nixon beauftragte seinen Stab, einen Plan zu entwickeln, um Ellsberg zu „neutralisieren". Man warb einen CIA-Agenten an und bildete eine Arbeitsgruppe, genannt „Plumber Unit" („Klempner"). Sie sollte verschiedene „kreative Ideen" umsetzen.

Zunächst ging man daran, in die Praxisräume des Psychiaters Fielding in Beverly Hills (Los Angeles) einzubrechen, bei dem Ellsberg einige Zeit in Behandlung gewesen war. Man hoffte, in den Patientenunterlagen geeignetes Material zu finden, um Ellsberg „anschwärzen" und diskreditieren zu können. Ziel war es, Ellsberg zum Schweigen zu bringen oder den Psychiater Fielding dafür zu gewinnen, gegen seinen Ex-Patienten als Zeuge auszusagen. Der Einbruch bei Fielding erwies sich jedoch als Fehlschlag, denn er erbrachte nicht das erhoffte Material.[20] Ein paar Monate später gelang es dem Weißen Haus, einige Exil-Kubaner zu rekrutieren, Veteranen aus der missglückten Invasion in der „Schweinebucht". Die Exil-Kubaner sollten Ellsberg „die Beine brechen".[21] Die vom Weißen Haus angeheuerten Schergen gaben jedoch vor Ort den ihnen aufgetragenen Plan auf, weil sie fürchteten, nach dem Anschlag auf Ellsberg nicht schnell genug entkommen zu können.

In der Zwischenzeit hatte das Weiße Haus den Richter Mathew Byrne, den Vorsitzenden im laufenden Strafverfahren gegen Daniel Ellsberg, in Nixons Haus nach San Clemente in Kalifornien eingeladen. Nixon und sein innenpolitischer Chefberater Ehrlichman boten Byrne im Verlaufe des Gesprächs sowie einige Tage danach nochmals den Posten des FBI-Direktors an.

Richter Byrne wurde am 27. April 1973 von den Ermittlungsbehörden in seiner Eigenschaft als Vorsitzender Richter im Strafverfahren gegen Ellsberg über den bereits erwähnten Einbruch der „Klempner" in die Praxis von Ellsbergs Psychiater Fielding in Kenntnis gesetzt. Neun Monate nach diesem Einbruch waren dieselben „Klempner" auch an dem Einbruch in das Hauptquartier der Demokratischen Partei im Washingtoner „Watergate"-Hotelkomplex beteiligt und wurden dafür strafrechtlich zur Verantwortung gezogen.[22]

Wenige Tage nach dem Eingehen des erwähnten Briefs erhielt Richter Byrne des Weiteren einen FBI-Report, in dem über das Geständnis des Chefberaters von Präsident Nixon (John Ehrlichman) berichtet wurde, den Einbruch in Fieldings Praxis angeordnet zu haben. Nach dem Bekanntwerden des FBI-Reports traten Ehrlichman und ein wei-

---

20 Ellsberg, Secrets, a.a.O, S. 460

21 Vgl. Ellsberg, Secrets, a.a.O., S. 468; Chalmers Johnson, The disquieted American, in: „The Guardian", 6.2.2003

22 Rudenstine, The Day the Presses Stopped, a.a.O., S. 347; Stanley I. Kutler, The Wars of Watergate: The Last Crisis of Richard Nixon. New York 1990, S. 254.

terer führender Mitarbeiter des Präsidenten zurück. Außerdem enthüllte der amtierende Chef der CIA, Richard Helms, dass die CIA auf Anordnung des Weißen Hauses ein Persönlichkeitsprofil Daniel Ellsbergs erstellt hatte, wozu die CIA nach dem Gesetz als Auslandsgeheimdienst keinesfalls berechtigt war.

Nun wurde es eng für Richter Byrne, dem ja vom Weißen Haus der Posten des immer noch vakanten FBI-Direktors mit dem offenkundigen Hintergedanken in Aussicht gestellt worden war, dass er sich dafür im Ellsberg-Strafverfahren im Sinne des Weißen Hauses erkenntlich zeigen würde. Unter dem Druck der Medien und der Öffentlichkeit sah Richter Byrne nur noch einen Ausweg, um nicht selbst – etwa wegen möglicher Bestechlichkeit – strafrechtlich verfolgt zu werden: Am 11. Mai 1973 gab er einem Antrag der Verteidigung statt – begründet mit den illegalen staatlichen Abhörmaßnahmen gegen Ellsberg in den Jahren 1969/70 –, die Anklage gegen Ellsberg fallen zu lassen und das Strafverfahren gegen ihn endgültig einzustellen.[23]

Die Veröffentlichung der „Pentagon Papers" und die damit verbundenen heftigen öffentlichen Auseinandersetzungen hatten in den USA Folgen von historischer Dimension. Zum einen waren sie ein außergewöhnlich wichtiger Beitrag dazu, das traditionelle blinde Vertrauen der Medien sowie großer Teile der US-Bevölkerung in die Glaubwürdigkeit ihres Präsidenten und der Regierung allgemein zu erschüttern. Denn nachlesbare Dokumente führten vor, in welchem Ausmaß demokratisch gewählte Regierungen unter den Präsidenten Truman, Eisenhower, Kennedy und Johnson zu Unwahrheiten, Lügen und „dirty tricks" bereit und in der Lage waren.

So hatten die „Pentagon Papers" die treibende Rolle aufgedeckt, die die US-Regierungen bei der völkerrechtswidrigen Boykottierung des Genfer Indochina-Abkommens und namentlich bei der Verhinderung allgemeiner Wahlen in Vietnam spielten. Die „Pentagon Papers" legten auch die politischen und kriminellen Verstrickungen der US-Regierung unter Präsident Kennedy in den Sturz und die Ermordung des südvietnamesischen Präsidenten Diem im Jahre 1963 bloß.[24] Sie enthüllten ferner die dreisten Schwindeleien und Täuschungen von Präsident Johnson im Zusammenhang mit dem von der US-Ma-

---

23 Vgl. Rudenstine, The Day the Presses stopped, a.a.O., S. 342; Ellsberg, Secrets, a.a.O., S. 467; Friedrich Karl Kaul, Watergate. Ein Menetekel für die USA, 2. Aufl. Berlin 1977, S. 144.
24 Die vor kurzem für diese Zeit freigegebenen Akten der US-Regierung bestätigen dies; vgl. die Nachweise auf der Homepage des „National Security Archive" an der George Washington University, Washington, www.nsarchive.org/NSAEBB/101/index.htm.

rine provozierten Scharmützel mit nordvietnamesischen Schiffen in der Tonking-Bucht im Jahre 1965. Durch diese Unwahrheiten und Täuschungen gelang es dem Präsidenten in verfassungswidriger Weise, eine parlamentarische Ermächtigung durch den US-Kongress zur völkerrechtswidrigen Bombardierung Hanois zu erlangen.

Durch die „Pentagon Papers" wurden aber auch zahlreiche weitere kleine und große Lügen der Exekutive gegenüber dem US-Kongress sowie der Öffentlichkeit über den Umfang, die Zielrichtung sowie die Auswirkungen des militärischen Engagements der USA in Vietnam bekannt. Publik wurden Strukturen im Apparat der Exekutive, die die jahrelange Verschleierung der amerikanischen Truppenpräsenz in Vietnam und der völkerrechtswidrigen Kriegsführung gefördert hatten. Offenkundig wurde auch das Ausmaß der stümperhaften und letztlich grob fehlerhaften Planungen und Entscheidungen des jeweiligen Präsidenten und seines Apparats während der gesamten Dauer der amerikanischen Intervention in Indochina: Man baute eine „Drohkulisse" auf, setzte seine eigene Glaubwürdigkeit aufs Spiel und sah dann zur Wahrung derselben nur noch die Eskalation als angemessenes Mittel – ein Stoff, den die amerikanische Historikerin Barbara Tuchman 1984 zu ihrem Buch „Die Torheit der Regierenden" verarbeiten sollte.

Die durch die Publizierung der „Pentagon Papers" erfolgte „Entzauberung" von Regierungshandeln – der Präsidenten-Kaiser stand plötzlich gleichsam „ohne Kleider" da – übertrug sich auch auf die innenpolitischen Auseinandersetzungen in den Vereinigten Staaten über die Vietnam-Kriegspolitik. Eine zunehmende Mehrheit der Bevölkerung und in den Medien wollte, nachdem man von den „Pentagon Papers" und den dadurch ausgelösten Kontroversen Kenntnis genommen hatte, Nixon und Co. einfach nichts mehr abnehmen. Man glaubte ihnen insbesondere nicht, dass sie den Krieg in Südostasien baldmöglichst beenden wollten. Denn das Töten und Sterben in Vietnam, in Laos und in Kambodscha ging derzeit ungeachtet aller Wahlkampfversprechen weiter.

Die Anti-Vietnamkriegs-Bewegung nutzte den Stimmungsumschwung und verstärkte ihn. Sie erfuhr im Gefolge der Auseinandersetzungen um die „Pentagon Papers" mit ihren fantasievollen Massenaktionen einen ungeheuren Auftrieb – national wie international. Sogar im US-Kongress gelang es, bei Resolutionen und bei Haushaltsberatungen von Fall zu Fall Mehrheiten gegen den Krieg zu organisieren. Die Massenmedien trugen ebenso zur Delegitimierung des Krieges bei, bis schließlich das Waffenstillstands-Abkommen ausgehandelt und unterzeichnet wurde und die US-Truppen aus Vietnam abzogen.

Die Lektionen der „Pentagon Papers"

Aus Daniel Ellsbergs Whistleblowing im Zusammenhang mit den „Pentagon Papers" lassen sich über die historischen Folgen seines Wirkens hinaus einige verallgemeinerungsfähige Erkenntnisse gewinnen, auf die Ellsberg selbst immer wieder hingewiesen hat.

Auch in demokratischen Staaten, und offenkundig nicht nur in den USA, ist Machtausübung und damit insbesondere auch das Kriegführen regelmäßig mit kleinen und großen Lügen sowie mit „dirty tricks" verbunden. Sie werden eingesetzt, um Journalisten, die Bevölkerung sowie die Parlamente zu gewinnen. Das haben auch in jüngster Zeit die Erfahrungen etwa mit der offiziellen Desinformationspolitik der beteiligten Entscheidungsträger im Golfkrieg 1991, während des Luftkrieges der NATO gegen Jugoslawien im Frühjahr 1999 sowie im Zusammenhang mit dem Krieg der „Koalition der Willigen" gegen den Irak im Frühjahr 2003 eindringlich bestätigt.

Die staatlichen Entscheidungsstrukturen und -prozesse werden dabei zugleich tunlichst gegen Einblicke und Kritik „von außen" abgeschottet. Potentielle Kritiker sollen von Informationen fern gehalten und abgeschnitten werden. Die von Nixon, Kissinger und anderen gegen die Publizierung der „Pentagon Papers" und für diese Abschottung ins Feld geführten Gesichtspunkte,[25] nämlich insbesondere die „nationale Sicherheit" sowie das Interesse ausländischer Verhandlungspartner an der Wahrung der Vertraulichkeit, können aber jedenfalls bei Verfassungsbrüchen oder schweren Völkerrechtsverletzungen keinen Vorrang beanspruchen. Verfassungsbrüche oder schwere Völkerrechtsverletzungen dürfen in einem demokratischen Rechtsstaat niemals Bestandteil von „nationaler Sicherheit" sein; sie verdienen auch im diplomatischen Verkehr keinen Schutz. Dies muss auch ausländischen Verhandlungspartnern klar sein – und notfalls durch Whistleblowing deutlich gemacht werden.

Mit der Abschottung nach „außen" – die „Pentagon Papers" belegen dies – geht in der Regel auch eine innere Verkrustung einher. Die Fähigkeiten und die Bereitschaft des politischen Systems zur Aufnahme von Kritik, die von „außen" kommt, gehen zurück. Die „Lernfähigkeit" des politischen Systems nimmt ab.[26] Nur selten finden sich Entschei-

---

25 Richard M. Nixon, The Memoirs of Richard Nixon, New York 1978, S. 511-514; Henry Kissinger, Years of Upheaval, Boston 1982, S. 115-117.
26 Vgl. zur Situation in den USA u.a. Daniel Ellsberg, The Presidential Decisions and Public Dissent, Institute of International Studies, University of California, Berkeley, 29.7.1998 (Interview mit Harry Kreisler).

dungsträger, die – wie etwa Robert McNamara – die Weitsicht und den Mut haben, die eigene Politik einer schonungslosen kritischen Bestandsaufnahme zu unterziehen sowie dafür die notwendigen Quellen und Akten wenigstens einer internen Arbeitsstelle bereitzustellen und sie mit dem erforderlichen Know-How und entsprechenden Kapazitäten auszustatten. Fehlt es an solchen Mechanismen zur Förderung und Gewährleistung der Lernfähigkeit und der Selbstreflexivität sowie zum effektiven „politischen Controlling" des politischen Systems, wächst die Bedeutung von Insidern, von Whistleblowern, die ab einem gewissen Stadium nicht mehr bereit sind, die „dirty tricks", die Verschleierungen und Lügen, sowie strukturelle Fehlleistungen des Apparates stillschweigend hinzunehmen oder sich gar zu Komplizen bei Gesetzes- und Verfassungsverstößen oder schweren Völkerrechtsverletzungen machen zu lassen.

Daniel Ellsberg hat diese Entwicklung durchlaufen. Er steht damit freilich nicht allein.[27] Nicht zuletzt die eingangs dargestellten aktuellen Whistleblower- Fälle im Zusammenhang mit dem Irakkrieg illustrieren dies. Sie unterstreichen die Bedeutung, die Whistleblowing als wichtigem Element einer „Verifikation durch die Zivilgesellschaft"[28] gerade auch in der Außen- und Sicherheitspolitik zukommt. Bürger und Bürgerinnen müssen dabei hinreichend geschützt werden, wenn sie Verstöße gegen internationale Abkommen der zuständigen Stelle anzeigen oder gar die Öffentlichkeit informieren. Konzepte einer solchen „gesellschaftlichen Verifikation" („societal verification") werden seit Jahrzehnten unter verschiedenen Bezeichnungen („Citizens' Reporting", „Inspection by the People", „Social Monitoring") diskutiert. Erste Ansätze für deren Umsetzung gibt es.[29] Hinreichende Schutzregelungen für Whistleblower existieren auf diesem Feld bislang jedoch nicht.

---

27 Vgl. die Angaben in: Dieter Deiseroth, Societal verification: wave of the future?, in: Trevor Findlay (Ed.), Verification Yearbook 2000, London 2000, S. 268 f.

28 Vgl. Joseph Rotblat, Societal Verification, in: J.Rotblat/J. Steinberger und B. Udgaonkar (Eds.), A Nuclear-Weapon-Free-World: Desirable? Feasible?, Colorado 1998, S. 112; – see above in this book p. 12 ff –

29 Vgl. Deiseroth, Societal Verification, a.a.O., S. 270 ff; ders., Zivilcourage am Arbeitsplatz – „Whistleblowing", in: Gerd Meyer, Ulrich Dovermann, Siegfried Frech und Günther Gugel (Hg.), Zivilcourage lernen, Bonn 2004, S.130 ff.

The German "Lex Ossietzky"

In his periodical *Die Weltbühne*, the German Nobel Peace Prize Laureate Carl von Ossietzky, a journalist and writer in the 1920s and 1930s, disclosed secret military co-operation (especially concerning the development of an illegal German airforce) between the German army and the Soviet authorities, which violated the international agreements concerning disarmament measures in the 1919 Versailles Peace Treaty. Though he and his defence counsels argued that his disclosure was justified by law because he disclosed "illegal state secrets" he was convicted of treason and espionage by the German Supreme Court ("Reichsgericht"; verdict of 13th of November 1931) and imprisoned.

In the 1960s, after a long and controversial debate on the necessary consequences of the "Ossietzky-Case" and on the lessons to be learned, the German Criminal Code (Strafgesetzbuch) was amended; in 1968 the German parliament passed a special clause concerning the problem of illegal state secrets.

Since then the German Criminal Code includes an article (Section 93 par. 2) that by itself can authorize, support, and justify whistleblowing for instance in the arms industry, in administration, in the military and in research and development agencies. The article can be summed up as the following: facts which constitute violations of international arms control agreements by virtue of having been kept secret from the treaty partners of Germany are not state secrets; disclosures of such illegal state secrets cannot be punished (unless Section 97a of the German Criminal Code is applicable). Thus, facts that violate international arms control agreements or disarmament treaties and which have been kept secret from the treaty partners of the Federal Republic of Germany can be reported to national and international verification authorities or to the general public by any citizen. A whistleblower who discloses such illegal state secrets shall not be punished as a traitor (Section 94), because of disclosure of state secrets (Section 95), because of treasonous espionage (Section 96) or because of revelation of state secrets (Section 97).

State secrets and illegal state secrets in the German Criminal Code (Strafgesetzbuch, StGB)

Official German version:

§ 93 Begriff des Staatsgeheimnisses

(1) Staatsgeheimnisse sind Tatsachen, Gegenstände oder Erkenntnisse, die nur einem begrenzten Personenkreis zugänglich sind und vor einer fremden Macht geheimgehalten werden müssen, um die Gefahr eines schweren Nachteils für die äußere Sicherheit der Bundesrepublik Deutschland abzuwenden.

(2) Tatsachen, die gegen die freiheitliche demokratische Grundordnung oder unter Geheimhaltung gegenüber den Vertragspartnern der Bundesrepublik Deutschland gegen zwischenstaatlich vereinbarte Rüstungsbeschränkungen verstoßen, sind keine Staatsgeheimnisse.

Translation provided by the Federal Ministry of Justice:

Section 93 Definition of State Secret

(1) State secrets are facts, objects or knowledge which are only accessible to a limited category of persons and must be kept secret from foreign powers in order to avert a danger of serious prejudice to the external security of the Federal Republic of Germany.

(2) Facts which constitute violations of the independent, democratic constitutional order or of international arms control agreements by virtue of having been kept secret from the treaty partners of the Federal Republic of Germany, are not state secrets.

Official German version:

§ 97a Verrat illegaler Geheimnisse

Wer ein Geheimnis, das wegen eines der in § 93 Abs. 2 bezeichneten Verstöße kein Staatsgeheimnis ist, einer fremden Macht oder einem ihrer Mittelsmänner mitteilt und dadurch die Gefahr eines schweren Nachteils für die äußere Sicherheit der Bundesrepublik Deutschland herbeiführt, wird wie ein Landesverräter (§ 94) bestraft. § 96 Abs. 1 in Verbindung mit § 94 Abs. 1 Nr. 1 ist auf Geheimnisse der in Satz 1 bezeichneten Art entsprechend anzuwenden.

Section 97a Betrayal of Illegal Secrets

Whoever communicates a secret, which is not a state secret because of one of the violations indicated in Section 93 subsection (2), to a foreign power or one of its intermediaries and thereby creates the danger of serious prejudice to the external security of the Federal Republic of Germany, shall be punished as a traitor (Section 94). Section 96 subsection (1), in conjunction with Section 94 subsection (1), no. 1, shall be correspondingly applicable to secrets of the type indicated in sentence 1.

Section 94 Treason

(1) Whoever:

1. communicates a state secret to a foreign power or one of its intermediaries; or

2. otherwise allows a state secret to come to the attention of an unauthorized person or to become known to the public in order to prejudice the Federal Republic of Germany or benefit a foreign power, and thereby creates a danger of serious prejudice to the external security of the Federal Republic of Germany,

shall be punished with imprisonment for not less than one year.

(2) In especially serious cases the punishment shall be imprisonment for life or for not less than five years. An especially serious case exists as a rule, if the perpetrator:

1. abuses a position of responsibility which especially obligates him to safeguard state secrets; or

2. creates by the act the danger of an especially serious prejudice to the external security of the Federal Republic of Germany.

Section 95 Disclosure of State Secrets

(1) Whoever allows a state secret, which has been kept secret by an official agency or at its behest, to come to the attention of an unauthorized person or become known to the public, and thereby creates the danger of serious prejudice to the external security of the Federal Republic of Germany, shall be punished with imprisonment from six months to five years if the act is not punishable under Section 94.

(2) An attempt shall be punishable.

(3) In especially serious cases the punishment shall be imprisonment from one year to ten years. Section 94 subsection (2), shall be applicable.

Section 96 Treasonous Espionage; Gathering Information About State Secrets

(1) Whoever obtain a state secret in order to betray it (Section 94), shall be punished with imprisonment from one year to ten years.

(2) Whoever obtains a state secret, which has been kept secret by an official agency or at its behest, in order to disclose it (Section 95), shall be punished with imprisonment from six months to five years. An attempt shall be punishable.

Section 97 Revelation of State Secrets

(1) Whoever allows a state secret, which has been kept secret by an official agency or at its behest, to come to the attention of an unauthorized person or become known to the public, and thereby negligently causes the danger of serious prejudice to the external security of the Federal Republic of Germany, shall be punished with imprisonment for not more than five years or a fine.

(2) Whoever recklessly allows a state secret, which has been kept secret by an official agency or at its behest and which was accessible to him by reason of his public office, government position, or assignment given by an official agency, to come to the attention of an unauthorized person, and thereby negligently causes the danger of serious prejudice to the external security of the Federal Republic of Germany, shall be punished with imprisonment for not more than three years or a fine.

(3) The act shall be prosecuted only with the authorization of the federal government.

Letter dated 17 December 2007 from the Permanent Representatives of Costa Rica and Malaysia to the United Nations addressed to the Secretary-General[*]

We have the honour to submit the enclosed document, which is an updated version of the Model Nuclear Weapons convention submitted by Costa Rica in 1997 and circulated by the Secretary-General of the United Nations as document A/C.1/52/7 (see annex). This revised model takes into account relevant technical, legal and political developments since 1997.

The Model Nuclear Weapons Convention has been drafted — and subsequently updated — by an international consortium of lawyers, scientists and disarmament experts. It is submitted as a work in progress setting forth legal, technical and political elements for the establishment and maintenance of a nuclearweapon-free world.

The existence of nuclear weapons and the possibility of nuclear proliferation continue to endanger all peoples and nations. These risks can be reduced and eliminated through the adoption of legally binding, verifiable and enforceable instruments culminating in a comprehensive prohibition and destruction of all nuclear weapons under effective controls.

The delegations submitting this Model Nuclear Weapons Convention do not suggest that an actual convention or package of agreements will exactly replicate this model. Rather, the Model Nuclear Weapons Convention is a useful tool in the exploration, development, negotiation and achievement of such an instrument or instruments.

The 1997 Model Nuclear Weapons Convention has assisted informal deliberations undertaken by governments, academics, technical experts, non-governmental organizations and others on the issues of, and possibilities for, nuclear disarmament. The delegations submitting this updated Model Nuclear Weapons Convention hope and expect that such deliberations will be stepped up in earnest and will evolve into actual negotiations.

---

[*]   *UN-Document A/62/650. 18 January 2008*

In this respect, we note the obligation affirmed by the International Court of Justice in 1996, to "pursue in good faith and bring to a conclusion negotiations on nuclear disarmament in all its aspects under strict and effective international control".

We note also the United Nations resolutions adopted annually since 1996 calling for the implementation of this obligation through "multilateral negotiations leading to an early conclusion of a nuclear-weapons convention prohibiting the development, production, testing, deployment, stockpiling, transfer, threat or use of nuclear weapons and providing for their elimination". Such negotiations can include the achievement of initial disarmament steps — whether unilateral, bilateral, plurilateral or multilateral — culminating in a convention or comprehensive package of instruments.

We kindly request you to have the present letter and the Model Nuclear Weapons Convention circulated as a document of the sixty-second session of the General Assembly, under agenda item 98.

(Signed) Jorge Urbina
Ambassador
Permanent Representative of Costa Rica to the United Nations

(Signed) Hamidon Ali
Ambassador
Permanent Representative of Malaysia to the United Nations

Model Nuclear Weapons Convention[*]

Chapter V. Verification

A. Elements of Verification Regime

In order to verify compliance with this Convention, a verification regime shall be established consisting of the following elements:

1. Agreements on sharing data and verification activities among States, UN organs and with existing agencies,
2. A Registry,
3. An International Monitoring System,
4. Reporting of information gathered by National Technical Means,
5. Open Skies,

---

*   ***Drafting Committee and Consultants:*** *Ed Aguilar Lawyers' Alliance for World Security, Glenn Alcalay NY Lawyers' Alliance for World Security, Frank Barnaby Oxford Research Group, Reiner Braun International Network of Engineers and Scientists for Global Responsibility, John Burroughs Western States Legal Foundation, Jackie Cabasso Western States Legal Foundation, Anne Marie Corominas Lawyers' Committee on Nuclear Policy, Merav Datan Lawyers' Committee on Nuclear Policy, Nicole Deller Lawyers' Committee on Nuclear Policy, Dieter Deiseroth International Association of Lawyers' Against Nuclear Arms, Anabel Dwyer Lawyers' Committee on Nuclear Policy, William Epstein Pugwash/NGO Committee on Disarmament Solange Fernex International Peace Bureau, Shirley Fingerhood Lawyers' Committee on Nuclear Policy, Tonya Frichner American Indian Law Alliance, Jonathan Granoff NGO Committee on Disarmament, Andre Gsponer Independent Scientific Research Institute, Rebecca Johnson Disarmament Intelligence Review, Martin Kalinowski International Network of Engineers and Scientists Against Proliferation, David Krieger Nuclear Age Peace Foundation, Kent Lebsock American Indian Law Alliance, Wolfgang Liebert International Network of Engineers and Scientists Against Proliferation, Pamela Meidell Abolition 2000 Global Network Office, Saul Mendlovitz Rutgers University School of Law/World Order Models Project, Elliot Meyrowitz Lawyers' Committee on Nuclear Policy, Pascale Norris Lawyers' Committee on Nuclear Policy, Douglas Roche Former Disarmament Ambassador for Canada, Daniel Plesch British American Security Information Council, Elizabeth Shafer Lawyers' Committee on Nuclear Policy, Jurgen Scheffran International Network of Engineers and Scientists Against Proliferation, Jonathan Schell Author, Victor Sidel International Physicians for the Prevention of Nuclear War, Alice Slater Global Resource Action Center for the Environment/Lawyers Alliance for World Security, Roger Smith NGO Committee on Disarmament, Kenji Urata Japanese Association of Lawyers Against Nuclear Arms, Carlos Vargas Foundation for the Development of International Law and Security, Paul Walker Former U.S. Congressional Aide, Alyn Ware Lawyers' Committee on Nuclear Policy, Lucy Webster Global Education Associates, Peter Weiss Lawyers' Committee on Nuclear Policy, Burns Weston University of Iowa College of Law*

6. Preventive controls,

7. Consultation and clarification,

8. On-site inspections, including challenge inspections,

9. Confidence-building measures, including additional voluntary measures,

10. Citizen and non-governmental reporting reporting and protection,

11. Any other measures deemed necessary by the Agency.

B. Activities, Facilities, and Materials Subject to Verification

12. All obligations of States Parties and persons as defined, inter alia, in Article I {General Obligations}, Article III {Declarations} and Article IV, Section D {Phases} shall be subject to verification in accordance with the relevant provisions of this Convention and its Verification Annex.

C. Rights and Obligations of States Parties with Respect to Verification

13. Verification activities shall be based on objective information, shall be limited to the subject matter of this Convention, and shall be carried out on the basis of full respect for the sovereignty of States Parties and in the least intrusive manner possible consistent with the effective and timely accomplishment of their objectives. Each State Party shall refrain from any abuse of the right of verification.

14. Each State Party undertakes in accordance with this Convention to cooperate through its National Authority established pursuant to Article VI {National Implementation Measures} of this Convention, with the Agency, with other States Parties and with other agencies as stipulated in this Convention and in separate agreements to facilitate the verification of compliance with this Convention by, inter alia:

a. Establishing the necessary facilities, or providing necessary modifications to existing facilities, to participate in these verification measures, and establishing the necessary communication;

b. Providing all relevant data obtained by technical means and by national systems that are part of the International Monitoring System as agreed among States;

c. Participating, as necessary, in a consultation and clarification process;

d. Permitting the conduct of on-site inspections;

e. Participating in confidence-building measures; and

f. To the extent possible, internationalizing elements of its National Technical Means and incorporating them into the International Monitoring System.

15. Each State Party shall have the right to take measures not contrary to the provisions of this Convention to prevent disclosure of confidential information and data not related to this Convention.

16. Subject to paragraph 15, information obtained by the Agency through the verification regime established by this Convention shall be made available to all States Parties in accordance with the relevant provisions of this Convention.

17. The provisions of this Convention shall not be interpreted as restricting the international exchange of data for scientific purposes not prohibited by this Convention.

18. Each State Party undertakes to cooperate with the Agency and with other States Parties in the improvement of the verification regime and in the examination of additional monitoring technologies. Such measures shall, when agreed, be incorporated in amendments to this Convention or changes to the Annexes or, where appropriate, be reflected in the operational manuals of the Technical Secretariat.

D. Confidence-Building Measures

19. Each State Party undertakes to cooperate with the Agency and with other States Parties in implementing various measures additional to those explicitly required under this Convention in order to:

a. Develop greater confidence regarding compliance with the obligations under this Convention, and
b. Assist in the compilation of detailed information by the International Monitoring System.

E. Relation to Other Verification Arrangements

20. The Technical Secretariat may enter into cooperative verification arrangements in accordance with the provisions of Article XIV {Cooperation, Compliance and Dispute Settlement} para. 3 and the provisions of Article XVIII, Section A {Relation to Other International Agreements} para. 2.

21. Nothing in this Convention shall be interpreted as in any way limiting or detracting from the verification arrangements assumed by either State under the Treaties Between the United States of America and the Russian Federation on Reduction and Limitation of Strategic Offensive Arms and the Treaty Between the United States of America and the Russian Federation on the Elimination of Their Intermediate-Range and Shorter-Range Missiles {INF}.

22. Nothing in this Convention shall be interpreted as in any way limiting or detracting from the verification arrangements assumed by Argentina and Brazil under the Agreement on the Exclusively Peaceful Use of Nuclear Energy.

23. Nothing in this Convention shall be interpreted as in any way limiting or detracting from the verification arrangements, assumed by any State under the Comprehensive Nuclear Test Ban Treaty, or under safeguards agreements and additional protocol agreements with the International Atomic Energy Agency [or under the Fissile Materials Cut-Off Treaty].

F. Implementation

24. Prior to entry into force of this Convention, nothing shall preclude any signatory State from implementing, individually or in agreement with other States, the verification measures of this Convention which are applicable to them. Such measures may include public declarations as detailed in Article III {Declarations}, negotiations with other States for the purposes of verifying bilateral or multilateral reductions of nuclear weapons, and the verification of plans for the destruction of nuclear weapons, disposition of special nuclear material, and destruction or conversion of nuclear weapons facilities or nuclear weapons delivery vehicles.

25. Verification measures adopted pursuant to paragraph 23 may include the formation of a provisional authority for the purpose of overseeing verification activities, including assistance in the development of national implementation plans pursuant to Article VI {National Implementation Measures} of this Convention.

Chapter VI. National Implementation Measures

A. Legislative Implementation

1. Each State Party shall, in accordance with its constitutional processes, adopt the necessary legislative measures to implement its obligations under this Convention. In particular, it shall:

a. Extend its penal legislation to provide, in accordance with Article VII, Section A, for the trial, extradition and punishment of persons who commit crimes as defined in Article I, Section B.
b. Provide all necessary protection for persons who report violations of this Convention, in accordance with Article VII, Section C.

2. Each State Party shall cooperate with other States Parties in affording legal assistance toward fulfilling the obligations under paragraph 1.

3. Each State Party, in the implementation of its obligations under this Convention, shall assign the highest priority to ensuring the safety of people and to protecting the environment, and shall cooperate as appropriate with other States Parties in this regard.

B. Relations Between the State Party and the Agency

4. In order to fulfill its obligations under this Convention, each State Party shall designate or establish a National Authority to serve as the national focal point for effective liaison with the Agency and other States Parties. Each State Party shall notify the Agency of its National Authority at the time that this Convention enters into force for it. The responsibilities of the National Authority include:

a. The preparations and submission of declarations in the registry;
b. The enactment of new legislation or the revision of existing legislation to facilitate the enforcement of the Convention;
c. Preparations for receiving inspections, including, inter alia, approval of the list of inspectors, issuing of multiple entry visas for inspectors, providing aircraft clearances, and designating points of entry and exit.

5. Each State Party shall inform the Agency of the legislative and administrative measures taken to implement this Convention.

6. Each State Party undertakes to cooperate with the Agency in the exercise of all its functions and in particular to provide assistance to the Technical Secretariat. This includes cooperation in carrying out any investigation which the Agency may initiate, and to provide or support assistance with investigations of non-complying State Parties and with Parties exposed to danger as a result of violation of this Convention.

7. Each State Party shall disseminate information regarding the requirements of this Convention and shall ensure the inclusion of such information in the training of relevant personnel regarding obligations under this Convention.

8. Each State Party shall transmit relevant information gathered by its National Technical Means to the International Monitoring System.

C. Confidentiality

9. Each State Party shall treat as confidential and afford special handling to information and data that it receives in confidence from the Agency. Information subject to confidentiality shall include data used for purposes not prohibited under this Convention and state and military technology for dual use vehicles, components and computers.

D. Relation to implementation measures assumed or required under other arrangements

10. Nothing in this Convention shall be interpreted as in any way limiting or detracting from the National Implementation Measures assumed or required by States under the Comprehensive Test Ban Treaty, International Atomic Energy Agency Safeguards agreements, International Convention for the Suppression of Acts of Nuclear Terrorism, [Fissile Materials Cut-Off Treaty] and United Nations Security Council resolution 1540.

Chapter VII. Rights and Obligations of Persons

A. Criminal Procedure

1. Any person accused of committing a crime under this Convention within the jurisdiction of a State Party of which such person is a citizen or resident shall be

a. tried according to the legal process of such State if found within such State, or
b. surrendered to the International Criminal Court if the crime alleged is within the jurisdiction of such Court and the State concerned is unable or unwilling to undertake adequate criminal procedures.

2. If found within another State Party, such person shall be

a. tried within such State, or
b. extradited to the State within the jurisdiction of which the crime is alleged to have been committed, or
c. surrendered to the International Criminal Court if the crime alleged is within the jurisdiction of such Court and the States concerned are unable or unwilling to undertake adequate criminal procedures.

3. Any person accused of a crime under this Convention shall be assumed to be innocent until proven guilty and have the right to a fair trial and humane treatment, as prescribed by the International Covenant on Civil and Political Rights and other conventions and agreements which have acquired the status of customary international law.

B. Responsibility to Report Violations

4. Persons shall report any violations of this Convention to the Agency. This responsibility takes precedence over any obligation not to disclose information which may exist under national security laws or employment contracts.

5. [Information received by the Agency under the preceding paragraph shall be held in confidence until formal charges are lodged, except to the extent necessary for investigative purposes.]

C. Protection for Persons Providing Information

Intra-state protection

6. Any person reporting a suspected violation of this Convention, either by a person or a State, shall be guaranteed full civil and political rights including the right to liberty and security of person.
7. States Parties shall take all necessary steps to ensure that no person reporting a suspected violation of this Convention shall have any rights diminished or privileges withdrawn as a result.
8. Any individual who [in good faith] provides the Agency or a National Authority with information regarding a known or suspected violation of this Convention cannot be arrested, prosecuted or tried on account thereof.

9. It shall be an unlawful employment practice for an employer to discriminate against any employee or applicant for employment because such person has opposed any practice as a suspected violation of this Convention, reported such violation to the Agency or a National Authority, or testified, assisted, or participated in any manner in an investigation or proceeding under this Convention.

10. Any person against whom a national decision is rendered on account of information furnished by such person to the Agency about a suspected violation of this Convention may appeal such decision to the Agency within [..] months of being notified of such decision. The decision of the Agency in the matter shall be final.

Inter-State Protection

11. Any person reporting a violation of this Convention to the Agency shall be afforded protection by the Agency and by all States Parties, including, in the case of natural persons, the right of asylum in all other States Parties if their safety or security is endangered in the State Party in which they permanently or temporarily reside.

Additional Provisions

12. [The Executive Council may decide to award monetary compensation to persons providing important information to the Agency concerning violations of this Convention.]

13. Any person who voluntarily admits to the Agency having committed a violation of this Convention, prior to the receipt by the Agency of information concerning such violation from another source, may be exempt from punishment. In deciding whether to grant such exemption, the Agency shall consider the gravity of the violation involved as well as whether its consequences have not yet occurred or can be reversed as a result of the admission made.

Civil Society's Contribution to CTBT Verification

Annegret Falter[1], Dieter Deiseroth[2], Martin B. Kalinowski[3].

[1] Freelance science journalist
[2] Bundesverwaltungsgericht Leipzig
[3] Carl Friedrich von Weizsäcker Center for Science and Peace Research, University of Hamburg, Germany,   * Corresponding Author

Universität Hamburg

Introduction

Societal Verification was conceived as a system of monitoring compliance with treaties, and detecting attempts to violate them, by:
• inducing civil society's actors to report to an international authority any information about attempted violation going on in their countries;
• making all such reporting become the right and the responsibility of all citizens;
• making that right becomes an explicit part of the national codes of law in the countries party to the treaty.   (Rotblat, 1993)

Societal Verification in the Model Nuclear Weapons Convention

Chapter VII (Rights and Obligation of Persons) defines an individual responsibility to report on violations of the Convention. In addition, it lists eight provisions for the protection of persons providing information on both intra- and inter-State level.

On 18 January 2008, the UN Secretary-General has circulated the model Nuclear Weapons Convention as UN Document No. A/62/650 to all UN member States at the request of Costa Rica and Malaysia.

Datan, M.; Hill, F.; Scheffran, J.; Ware, A.; Kalinowski, M.; Seidel, V.: Securing our Survival (SOS). The Case for a Nuclear Weapons Convention. IPPNW, IALANA and INESAP. Cambridge, Massachusetts 2007.

Technical means enabling civil society verification

Any Citizen who happens to be close to a testing ground can use:

Photo, video and audio equipment

Specialized technical experts can use:

• Scientific and open source seismic raw data and event analysis
• Commercial or open source multispectral images from satellites
• Open source satellite radar images
• Atmospheric radioactivity measurements in conjunction with open source atmospheric transport modeling

Historical Precedences

A large proportion of the more than 2050 historic nuclear weapons tests became known to the public.

• Seismic analysis revealed most underground test.
• Radionuclide debris indicated atmospheric tests and venting from underground nuclear explosions.
• Satellite image analysis was conducted on all major testing areas.
• Satellite radar interferometry was applied to the Nevada test site.

As a result, within one day nuclear tests were in the news and public pressure groups protested promptly.

Role of the civil society in CTBT verification

Data analysis related to the North Korean nuclear explosion of 2006 demonstrated that the international civil society has access to data and information though the official CTBT verification system is open to authorized governmental members only.
Though it is extremely unlikely that a nuclear test remains undetected by the official verification system, civil society has an important role in

• Revealing internal information beforehand (by whistle-blowing or citizen's reporting);
• Providing additional data and analysis for threat assessment, for the political decision making process and a targeted conduct of Onsite Inspections;
• Creating worldwide transparency and public debate on suspicious events;
• Counterbalancing biased verification findings.

Example

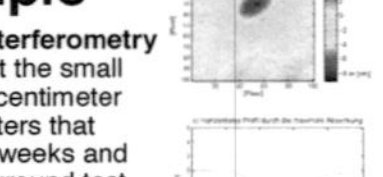
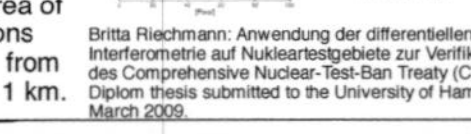

Differential radar interferometry can be used to detect the small subsidence of a few centimeter over hundreds of meters that follow within the first weeks and years after an underground test. This can result in an event location that reduces the area of interest for Onsite Inspections down from about 1000 km from seismic analysis to around 1 km.

Britta Riechmann: Anwendung der differentiellen SAR-Interferometrie auf Nukleartestgebiete zur Verifikation des Comprehensive Nuclear-Test-Ban Treaty (CTBT). Diplom thesis submitted to the University of Hamburg, March 2009.

Societal Verification provisions in existing nuclear arms control

In humanitarian arms control and particularly in the Ottawa Convention banning anti-personnel mines, the civil society plays a constitutional role. Though a comparable influence cannot be expected for nuclear arms control, more than is current practice is possible and desirable.

Legal protection mechanisms in support of societal verification

1. While Article III of the CTBT deals in general terms with national implementation measures it does not specify what measures are to be taken by the States Parties, or how. It is for each State Party to decide what measures, in accordance with its constitutional processes, would be appropriate. These measures should include provisions to ensure that any individual who in good faith provides the CTBTO or the appropriate national authority with information regarding a known or suspected violation of the CTBT
• cannot be arrested, prosecuted or tried on account thereof
• shall be guaranteed full civil and political rights including the right to liberty and security of person; no such person shall have any rights diminished or privileges withdrawn as a result.

2. Any person reporting (in good faith) a suspected violation of the CTBT to the CTBTO or any appropriate national authority shall be afforded protection by the CTBTO and by all States Parties, including the right of asylum in all other States Parties if his or her safety or security is endangered in the State Party in which he or she permanently or temporarily resides. According to Art. II Sec. D par. 43 (g) the Technical Secretariat of the CTBTO, subject to prior approval by the Executive Council, shall negotiate such provisions in appropriate agreements or arrangements with States Parties or other States.

Summary

To the extent that technical verification measures, applied by states or international organizations, ma y provide unsatisfying results, societal verification could gain importance, in particular if based on new technologies. Societal verification could complement official verification, and even more so if whistle blowing and citizens reporting on breaches of contract are explicitly protected by law.
Verification Agencies should not only be authorized to use open source information, but also be obliged to publish the results of compliance monitoring.

Carl Friedrich von Weizsäcker Centre for Science and Peace Research

Beim Schlump 83
20144 Hamburg
Germany

Tel. +49 40 42838 4335
Fax. +49 40 42838 3052
http://www.ZNF.uni-hamburg.de
Martin.Kalinowski@uni-hamburg.de

Supported by:

Deutsche Stiftung Friedensforschung

German Foundation for Peace Research

References:

Ronald B. Mitchell. Identifying Undeclared Nuclear Sites: Contributions from Nontraditional Sources: In 2nd Workshop on Science and Modern Technology for Safeguards: Proceedings (Albuquerque, NM, 21-24 September 1998). Editors: C. Foggi and E. Petraglia. Office for Official Publications of the European Communities, 2000, 59-72.

Joseph Rotblat, Societal Verification, in: J. Rotblat, J. Steinberger, B. M. Udgaonkar, A Nuclear-Weap on-Free World: Desirable? Feasible?, Boulder: Westview Press, 1993. "The concept of citizen's reporting has been discussed in the literature for many years, under different names, such as 'inspection by the people', or 'knowledge detection'. The idea was introduced in the late 1950s by Lewis Bohn and Seymour Melman and incorporated in the classic World Peace Through World Law by Grenville Clark and Louis Sohn. Leo Szilard, in his quixotic The Voice of the Dolphins also considered it an important part of the disarmament process."

Dieter Deiseroth, Societal Verification, BoD., Delmenhorst 2008 (ISBN 978-3-8370-6582-4).

Dieter Deiseroth, Societal Verification: Wave of the Future, in: Verification Yearbook 2000 (ISBN 1-89 9548- ISSN 1355-5847).

Select Bibliography

Arendt, Hannah: Lying in Politics, first published in: The New York Review of Books, 18th of November 1971. Reprinted in: Hannah Arendt, Wahrheit und Lüge in der Politik. Zwei Essays. München 1972, p. 7 - 43

Arndt, Adolf: Landesverrat. Luchterhand Verlag. Berlin/Neuwied. 1966

Bohn, Lewis: Tecniche d'ispezione non materiale *in: Brennan, Donald G.(ed.):* Controlli degli armamenti, disarmo e sicurezza nazionale, New York/Milan. 1961

Burroughs, John: Legal and policy bases for citizen verification of the elimination of nuclear, chemical, and biological weapons. (see: http://www.lcnp.org/wcourt/L%20&%20 P%20Basis%20for%20Citizens%20Weapons%20Inspections.htm)

Calland, Richard and Dehn, Guy: Whistleblowing Around The World. Law, Culture and Practice. Published by The Open Democracy Advice Centre (ODAC). Cape Town (South Africa), 2004 (ISBN 1-919798-56-0)

Clark, Grenville and Sohn, Louis B.: World Peace through World Law (2nd ed.), Cambridge: Harvard University Press, 1962.
German Edition: *Clark, Grenville/Sohn, Louis B.:* Frieden durch ein neues Weltrecht. Hrsg. Von der Forschungsstelle für Völkerrecht und ausländisches öffentliches Recht der Universität Hamburg und übersetzt von Claus Weiß. Alfred Metzner Verlag. Frankfurt/Main und Berlin. 1. Auflage. 1961

Cohen, Yoel: Nuclear Ambiguity – The Vanunu Affair. Sinclair-Stevenson. London. 1992. German Edition: Palmyra Verlag. Heidelberg. 1995 (ISBN 3-930378-03-5)

Deiseroth, Dieter: Berufsethische Verantwortung in Forschung. Möglichkeiten und Grenzen des Rechts. LIT-Verlag. Münster. 1997 (ISBN 3-8258-3160-4)

Deiseroth, Dieter/Göttling, Dietmar (Ed.): Der Fall Nikitin – The Nikitin Case. G.Emde Verlag. Pittenhart. 2000 (ISBN 3-923637-56X)

Deiseroth, Dieter: Whistleblowing in Zeiten von BSE. Berlin Verlag. Berlin. 2001 (ISBN 3-8305-0258-3)

Deiseroth, Dieter/Falter, Annegret: Whistleblower Preis 2003 – Daniel Ellsberg. Berlin Verlag. Berlin. 2004 (ISBN 3-8305-0973-1)

Deiseroth, Dieter/Falter, Annegret: Whistleblower in Gentechnik und Rüstungsforschung – Preisverleihung 2005 an Theodore A. Postol und Arpad Pusztai. Berlin Verlag. Berlin. 2005 (ISBN 3-8305-0973-1)

Deiseroth, Dieter: Der offene und freie Diskurs als Voraussetzung verantwortlicher Wissenschaft, in: *Albrecht, Stefan/ Braun, Reiner / Held, Thomas (Ed.):* Einstein weiterdenken. Thinking Beyond Einstein. Peter Lang Verlag. Frankfurt/Main. 2006 (ISBN 3-631-55228-9), p. 193 - 225

Deiseroth, Dieter/Falter, Annegret: Whistleblower in Altenpflege und Infektionsforschung – Preisverleihung 2007 an Brigitte Heinisch und Liv Bode. Berlin Verlag. Berlin. 2007 (ISBN 978-3-8305-1455-8)

Devine, Tom: The Whistleblower's Survival Guide. Courage Whithout Martyrdom. Published by the Fund for Constitutional Government. Washington DC 1997

Ellsberg, Daniel: Papers On The War. Simon and Schuster, New York, 1972

Ellsberg, Daniel: Secrets. A Memoir Of Vietnam And The Pentagon Papers. Viking Penguin Books. London. 2002 (ISBN 0-670-03030-9)

Findlay, Trevor (Ed.): Verification Yearbook 2000. The Verification Research, Training and Information Center (Vertic), London. 2000 (ISBN 1-899548-21-1)

Goldblat, Jozef: Arms Control. The New Guide to Negotiations and Agreements. Fully Revised and Updated Second Edition. PRIO Sipri. SAGE Publications. London. 2002 (ISBN 0 7619 4015 4)

Hartung, Aurica: Geheimnisschutz und Whistleblowing im deutschen und englischen Recht. VDM Verlag Dr. Müller. Saarbrücken. 2006 (ISBN 3-86550-101-X)

IPPNW/IALANA/INESAP (Ed.): Sicherheit und Überleben. Argumente für eine Nuklearwaffenkonvention. Berlin 2000 (ISBN 3-00-006743-4)

Kohlmann, Günter: Der Begriff des Staatsgeheimnisses und das verfassungsrechtliche Gebot der Bestimmtheit von Strafvorschriften. Verlag Dr. Otto Schmidt KG. Köln. 1969

Meier, Oliver / Tenner, Clare: Non-governmental monitoring of international agreements, in: Verification Yearbook 2001, Edited by *Trevor Findlay and Oliver Meier.* VERTIC, London, 2001, (ISBN 1-899548-32-7), p. 207 - 222

Melman, Seymour: General Report, in: *Seymour Melmon (ed.):* Inspection for Disarmament. Columbia University Press, New York. 1958, p. 38

Newcombe, Hanna: Citizen Reporting as a Method of Arms Control Verification, in: Hans Günter Brauch (Ed.): Weapons Technology, Disarmamentand Verification IPRA Defense and Disarmament Study Group Paper 1. AFES-PRESS Report No. 41 1991, 141pp. (ISBN 3-926979-36-4)

Ossietzky, Carl von: 227 Tage im Gefängnis. Briefe, Texte, Dokumente. Luchterhand Literatur Verlag. Darmstadt. 1988 (ISBN 3-630-86670-0)

Politi, Marco: Diritto Internazionale E Non Proliferazione Nucleare. Edizioni Cedam. Padova. 1984

Portnoy, B.M.: `Arms Control Procedure: Inspection by the People - A Revaluation and a Proposal', Cornell International Law Journal, vol.4, no.2, 1971

Public Concern at Work (ed.): Current Law Statutes. Public Interest Disclosure Act 1998. Annotations by *Guy Dehn*, Legal Information Resources. Sweet & Maxwell. London. 1999.

Rotblat, Joseph: The Crime and Punishment of Mordechai Vanunu, in: Voices For Vanunu. Papers from the International Conference, Tel Aviv, October 1997. An International Symposium of Experts and Whistleblowers. Chaired by Professor Joseph Rotblat. R.A.P. Printers & Publishers. London. 1997 (ISBN 0-953131-30-0)

Rotblat, Joseph: Societal Verification, in: *Rotblat, Joseph/ Steinberger, Jack/ Udgaonkar, Bhalchandra (Ed.),* A Nuclear-Weapon-Free-World: Desirable? Feasible?, Westview Press, Boulder, Colorado, 1998, p. 112 pp

Weapons of Mass Destruction Commission: Weapons Of Terror. Freeing the World of Nuclear, Biological and Chemical Arms. Stockholm. 2006 (ISBN 91-38-22582-4)

Westman, Daniel P.: Whistleblowing. The Law of Retaliatory Discharge. The Bureau of National Affairs. Inc., Washington D.C. 1991 (ISBN 0-87179-661-9)